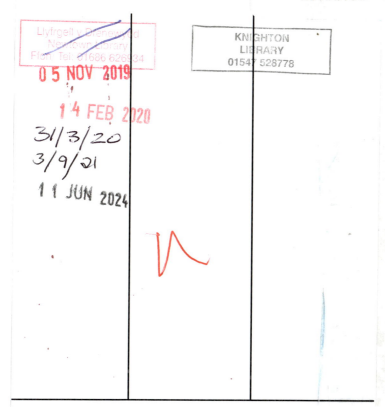

Dedicated to my father
Eric Valentine Baker
who started me off down the path of the Unexpected.

In Passing

A Welshman's
bizarre adventures
from Merthyr
to Mecca

RANDALL BAKER

y Lolfa

First impression: 2019

© Copyright Randall Baker and Y Lolfa Cyf., 2019

The contents of this book are subject to copyright, and may
not be reproduced by any means, mechanical or electronic,
without the prior, written consent of the publishers.

Cover illustration: Mumph
Text illustrations: Iva Tsankova

ISBN: 978 1 78461 722 6

Published and printed in Wales
on paper from well-maintained forests by
Y Lolfa Cyf., Talybont, Ceredigion SY24 5HE
website www.ylolfa.com
e-mail ylolfa@ylolfa.com
tel 01970 832 304
fax 832 782

Contents

Before You Start

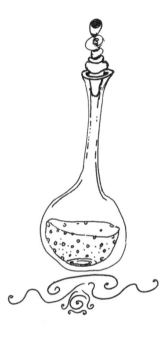

THERE ARE TWO questions to be addressed here, viz., "What's this all about?" and "Why should I read this?" Taking them in the order posed, I can only resort to repeating a phrase that has dogged me all my life, namely, "Why do these things always happen to you?" This has been posed for decades by the politer element among my friends. The less-believing are of the "Oh, come off it!" school of criticism, and resort to some variant of "You're making this up."

Chief amongst the heretics was my late wife, especially where stories about my brother were concerned,[1] frequently

---

1   None of which appear in here, but do stretch credulity to the limits. On the other hand, to paraphrase what they used to say in a long-running TV programme of the 1960s, *All things are as they were, but I was there.*

remarking in company apropos of some colourful reminiscence, "Oh, that's just one of his tales."

After we were married, she travelled with me to Wales, and encountered my brother de-hexing his car at midnight from a local witch's curse. She took me into the corridor and, looking alarmed, said, "You never told me these things were all *true!*" That moment of truth is offered to all the doubting Thomases out there.

So, the two elements in the book are: (a) there must be something worthwhile in these stories if people consistently challenge their veracity, so they may deserve a wider audience, and (b) they have stood the test of time, starting in the Welsh Valleys of the late 1940s and 1950s, and moving to Fiji and New Zealand in the 1980s and the State of Indiana in the mid 'Noughties'.

The real *theme*, since I suppose I am expected to have something to hold this book together, is the continual presence of the *unexpected*, and sometimes *inexplicable*, in my life – and I have assembled here but a small sample of such cases. Truly, some of these stories I simply *cannot* explain – I know only that they happened. Furthermore, the pervasive, rather oblique and offbeat Welsh way of looking at things and, worse, writing about them, must have a significant role in what follows. Truly, some of these episodes were totally disorienting or even alarming at the time (it is hard to find lightheartedness and wry wit in a double homicide in California, commonplace though they may be in that bizarre spot), but that's just the way it appears when I write it down – probably a 'Celtic thing'.

I confess, right away, to a lifelong fascination with the bizarre. No, I had better correct that word or it will spawn thousands of videos on YouTube. I mean, the truly unusual and anomalous, such as the fact that Spain has a town situated totally inside France; Germany and Italy have towns totally within Switzerland, and that, oddly, you have to go through Canada to get to two towns in different parts of the USA from the rest of the USA. Just how bad this affliction with anomaly can be is illustrated by the fact that, with my colleague Dr Roger Mallion, I spent 24 years researching why the Prussian-Dutch[2] border didn't meet for 100 years after 1815, leaving an entire town in a triangular no-man's land called the 'Neutral Territory'. This fascination resulted in a slim, though passably impressive, volume that elicited a comment from HM The King of the Belgians.[3]

That's as much as I can do by way of explanation – or was it *justification?* I am lucky to have worked in over 60 countries, adding a global flavour to what, at first, I took – parochially – to be the recurring weirdness of Wales. I still have no answer to the 'why me?' question in terms of the recurrence of these odd events, though I am very grateful for the everlasting interest these happenings have provided. Best of all, they continue.

Acknowledgements

My first thanks must go to the talented young Bulgarian artist Iva Tsankova. She provided all the artwork you see within these pages, and it will also be used in the Bulgarian-language edition of this book.

I'd also like to thank Mumph for his brilliant cover artwork. I think it conveys the bizarreness of the incidents contained in this book admirably!

My assistant, Liliya Hristova has kept me organised in not losing files or forgetting which book I am working on, my name, etc.

I have really enjoyed working with Y Lolfa, especially Carolyn Hodges, who oversaw the editing process, the de-Americanisation of the text, and the tossing overboard of

---

2   And later, in the same place, the Belgian-German border.
3   Randall Baker, Roger Mallion, *Moresnet. The Curious Complexities of a Neutral Zone*, Paradigma, 2010.

terms that I had not realised had now become archaic (like me, I suppose). Thanks also to Jen Llywelyn for her proofreading skills.

Finally, I have to thank Merthyr for a unique upbringing, including being educated in a castle.

Randall Baker
Tyn y Pant, Powys
April 2019

FIRST INSTALMENT

Being British

1

Train of thought

THOUGH MY FATHER could remember the configuration of the braking system on a 1922 Trojan car with wooden wheels, he rarely had much grasp of what had happened during the last 24 hours. Everyone learned to live with this situation, and knew that glasses, gloves, etc. had a half-life of about twenty minutes. He also should never have been allowed to travel by train, for reasons that will become obvious. In fact, I remember only two occasions when I travelled by train with him: the first time was in the 1950s going to London from the south of Wales. I recall that before departing the platform at Paddington, he tipped the driver of the huge green steam locomotive; something that I have never seen done since. The second time was slowly proceeding home from some business in central Wales. This journey was through the Brecon Beacons – one of the loveliest, and least known, landscapes in the country. The train was a 'local'; the locomotive, of course, being steam powered, and pulling only two very old carriages adorned with sepia prints of people in straw hats in Cornwall around the time of the War of 1914, or of brave viaducts along the route of Brunel's Great Western Railway – whose logo the carriages still bore. The whole journey had a bucolic timelessness that I remember to this day.

The pace was slow, as befitted the stately dignity of an earlier age: indeed, we could have disembarked and walked alongside much of the way, because it was a mighty climb through the mountains up to the Heads of the Valleys watershed, over which we would eventually have to go. There was a sense of being comfortably trapped in this already 150-year-old means of locomotion, and being required to abide by the mores of another age. My great-grandfather would have found nothing much different about the conditions of our journey that day, click-clacking along in our time capsule following the rails his contemporaries had laid through this wild and sweeping landscape. There was also something wonderfully anthropomorphic about the locomotive's laboured breathing as it struggled against the continual incline. But no one cared to go any faster; we had, perforce, nothing else to do but sit back and contemplate the wonders of nature, and feel a sense of common cause with the sheep that remained quite unmoved by our passage through their green domain. Furthermore, and I remember this well, the sun was shining – which alone, in Wales, should have burned the day into my memory. At every stop, my father descended to chat with the driver of this timeless beast (whose days were numbered until 1968, when the steam engine was hunted to extinction by 'Progress').

"Hot work, I imagine?" was how he opened the dialogue with the driver.

"It's a 'eck of a sight 'otter for 'im," the driver replied, pointing over his shoulder at the fireman moving coal from tender to firebox.

"Shuntin' see, that's what this tank engine is for, not bloody mountain-climbing, mun," the fireman remarked, popping up over the driver's shoulder. "Can't bloody stop shovellin' for a minute, mun. We're usin' every ounce see, every ounce," he emphasised, his face a mixture of sweat and coal dust.

"Well then, you'd better get back to it, boyo," the driver remarked, with a big wink at the two of us. "You've lost us about 2 lbs of ounces just standing there nattering."

You have to understand that for a child of my age at that time, there was nothing more awe-inspiring than the hissing, well-oiled, brass-bound magic that was a *locomotive*. The people who tamed and controlled this beast were magicians, and it was every boy's dream to be an engine driver. Of course, at that point, I had never seen an aeroplane or a steamship. So, as I stood in awe, the conversation continued. "Maybe if we walk alongside, it will relieve some of the strain and the fireman can have a bit of a rest?" my father enquired – his tone serious, but the squeeze of his hand on mine giving away the joke.

"No, that's alright. Not far now, better get in," came the voice of the fireman from somewhere near the jaws of Hell.

Although nothing particularly odd occurred when I travelled with him, things had a tendency to go decidedly awry, if not downright amok, when my father travelled alone by train. Well, actually, that is not entirely accurate, for had he been *strictly speaking* travelling *alone*, there would have been no problems. In each case, calamity resulted because an audience was present.

First, contrary to the *English* reticence about exchanging words with people to whom you have not been introduced – even if you are married to them – the Welsh have absolutely no problem with this. They size you up for a moment, then lead in with some opening line such as: "I see Swansea lost again. I wonder why they bother. It's rediclus."[4]

This approach does not work in England, and is actually not an ice-breaker so much as a way to provoke the onset of another glacial age. This random intrusion of different strangers into one's personal space is one of the hazards of using public transport, unless you are rich and can avoid the hoi polloi. But even then the nouveau riche can infiltrate if all it takes to do so is money.

My father simply had no sense of this. First of all, he rarely used public transport at the best of times and so, when he did, it was, as he would say, "a bit of an occasion". He did, once, however, manage to put public transport to good use without ever getting on board.

We were attempting to stay with old friends in Grays, Essex. My father's certainty about where they lived proved illusory, and eventually there we were in the car wandering the Essex marshes like some lost souls in an M R James story. God forbid, though, that we should give up and *ask* someone, or buy a map – no self-respecting man would do that, even now. My father was saying, "I'm absolutely sure that it is in this direction," when he suddenly engaged first gear and took us off in the *opposite* direction. Because of my worsening mood, I thought it best not to say anything. After his sudden change of direction, we continued driving for quite some time. And it was becoming really irritating, because he found it necessary to pull up every time the double-decker bus in front of us stopped.

"Look, you have a completely clear road, let's pass this filthy

---

4   The uniquely Welsh rendering of 'ridiculous'. I emphasise this because it is a word in very common use in south Wales. The other mutilated word to know is 'buwtiful", with the first syllable extended to three times the normal length. Most confusing of all is the expression "isn't it?", which actually means something like an emphasis of what you just said. "There's a lovely day, isn't it?" does not require an answer. "I'm going shopping now, isn't it?" not only does not require an answer – it boggles the mind to think what it might be.

thing," I exclaimed, for the bus was belching out black clouds of used diesel fuel.

"Can't do that, see," he said, drumming his fingers on the steering wheel.

"Why ever not?" I asked, because we could have passed the bus three times in the period it had taken to have this conversation.

He didn't answer, but just extended his finger toward the bus. I could not imagine what he meant until I realised that one of the destinations of this bus, displayed on the panel on the back, was *Grays*. It took a while, and our lungs were probably poisoned, but we arrived in time for lunch.

A falling out among passengers

It was in that very same county of Essex that one of father's greatest rail adventures began, but at a much earlier time – the late 1940s, in fact. He was in Dagenham, where the Ford Motor Company has a plant the size of a small country. Why he was there I have no idea, and since I was four, I don't suppose I asked. He was staying with the self-same friends who lived along the bus route mentioned above, but on this occasion, my father travelled each day by train from Grays to Dagenham and vice versa. Things were still pretty austere in that early post-War period, but at least he had the adventure of being in the big city.

As he travelled back each night with the other commuters, he became fascinated by one thing. The passengers seemed to know when to get off without even glancing out of the window. The train would start to slow down, at which signal they would fold their newspapers, put them in their briefcases, and pick up hats and umbrellas. Then they would line up behind the door, and then as the train shuddered to a stop they would step down, and walk determinedly out onto the platform without even the merest glance at the station name. My father, on the other hand, was provincially paranoid about missing his stop and checked every station platform name board along the way many times. So, of course, he was very intrigued to know how they did it. It began to nag at him.

He had plenty of time to work it out, travelling every evening during one of the worst winters ever recorded in Britain (1947). It is necessary to explain here the configuration of the carriage in which he sat each day. There was no corridor, either in the middle or at the side. The carriage was divided by a series of bulkheads into small compartments with two bench seats facing each other and a door at either side of the compartment.

By the time he boarded, many of the passengers were already in place and well into their newspaper. Each evening on the journey home he watched, and it began to drive him mad. How did they do it? He could not fathom this problem but was not going to rest until he had the answer, as is normal for the Welsh. Then he would no longer have to leap up every time the train stopped to see where he was. Unable to work it out, he knew that, eventually, he would *have* to ask.

And so he worked up the determination to do so, though he wanted to wait until it was just him and one other person, thus reducing the embarrassment for both parties.

Eventually, everything came together. It was a particularly bad night and the temperature was already well below freezing. Shivering passengers exited into the snow until, at last, there was only one person remaining in the compartment with him. He would do it – *now*.

He thought about how to approach the question, but while he was thinking about that, the switching points froze further up the track, which meant that my father's train could not move into its next section. There is no danger if this problem occurs, because the signal light that faces the train will remain red, and so the train cannot proceed.

Unaware of the mechanical problem ahead, my father leaned forward and opened his mouth to pose the big question. Before he could utter a single word, the train slowed down rather abruptly and stopped. The man folded his newspaper with military precision, picked up his briefcase, put on his hat, opened the door swiftly, and fell out onto the tracks.

My father watched all this with a sense of wonder, because he had clearly seen that they were in the middle of a frozen nowhere when the train slowed down. Now he would not be able to ask the question. In addition, the system had clearly not had all the kinks worked out of it after all, viz., the lemming passenger who had just dropped out of sight. While he was thinking about that, he suddenly realised that the hapless passenger might be in mortal danger. Or dead, which is *im*mortal danger, I suppose. So he jumped to his feet and peered down from the still-open door. There, below him, was the passenger, soaked, ashen-faced, covered in snow and dazed, but reassuringly still very much of this world, looking back at him.

"Here, give me your hand – you can't stay out there on the tracks," father said and extended his very strong arm. He more or less manhandled the city gent to the safety of the compartment, though the hat was definitely a casualty.

"Are you all right?" my father asked. "No bones broken, that sort of thing?"

The man gradually eased himself up from the floor onto the seat he had so recently vacated. He looked intact but very, very embarrassed.

"I can't imagine why I did that," he said, totally puzzled.

"Yes, but you are lucky. You could have been killed, you know – the fall, a passing train, and here we are, almost Christmas."

"Twenty-one years!" said the man, suddenly and loudly.

"Twenty-one years what?" my father enquired, confused.

"I have travelled this line for twenty-one years. Every working day. Why would I *now* do such a stupid thing?" His voice was coming close to the edge of hysteria.

"Now, calm down," my father said, realising that the train had not moved since this strange event occurred. "Just be thankful you survived it with no broken limbs."

But the embarrassed fellow was not to be pacified.

"Twenty-one years. It's ridiculous. Why? Why?" he said, gathering up his scattered belongings.

Then it occurred to my father, given the recent serious breakdown in the exiting strategy, that this might be just the right time to ask his question. But, the thought was moot because just then, to my father's continuing amazement, the man leapt up, dusted himself down, opened the door *on the other side*, and fell out – again. This time he did not return, but instead ran off up the track shouting, while my father, kneeling in the open door, watched him disappear. He had simply thought he had alighted on the wrong side.

"Now I will *never* know," he thought. Then he made a mental note: "I think I will stick to my method. I wonder where we are."

With that, the signal turned green, the train lurched off and my father closed the door but remained standing at the window, hoping to catch a glimpse of the dazed commuter as the train gradually overtook him.

The high price of socialism

My father ate tea with us, just not in the same room. When he arrived home, my mother and I would often already be seated around the kitchen table by the fireplace, so he would pick up a plate, collect his chosen items and disappear into the next room to watch the television news. Nevertheless, conversation continued despite our physical separation and lack of any line of sight.

During another bad winter my father was, once more, aboard a train. This time he had arrived home from Cardiff (about 20 miles away), and had selected his movable feast. Then, from the flickering darkness of the next room, we heard: "I am frozen solid. You can't imagine what a nightmare that train journey was. Can you believe this: there was *no* heating on that train. Absolutely nothing. And this is the middle of winter.

There were old ladies aboard that train, and they were feeling the cold very badly," he said, clearly very upset and angry.

My mother and I continued eating the Swiss roll as the story began from the next room. She listened as the drama unfolded, even though her attention was mainly focused on the crossword in front of her. The disembodied tale continued.

"It was like being in a fridge. So along comes the ticket inspector, and I said to him, 'Why is there no heating on this train?' He told us he had no idea how this had come about, and basically that it was not his responsibility. 'I only collect the tickets,' was his response. I mean, what an attitude. I told the ladies, 'You see, that is what happens when you hand over something to the state. When we had Great Western Railways, the system worked like clockwork *and* the trains were clean.' I can't imagine them sending us out to our deaths in an ice-box. That's what happens when nobody owns the firm. Nobody cares. 'It's not my job,' should be the government's motto. If there isn't someone in business at the top, we can all go to blazes. Just like this train, there should be inspections and maintenance, but nobody cares, so nobody thinks, and it's up to us to pay the price. The workers become like zombies, not paying attention and not thinking, not thinking at all."

Clearly this tirade had used up more energy than he had planned, since he came back to the table for a refill. Without looking up from a four-letter word meaning *beach apparel*, my mother said, "What I don't understand is what you were doing in the train at all. You went down there in the car."

She continued with 15 down as my father slipped back into the darkness of the TV room, which also contained the substantial black Bakelite telephone. This now earned its keep by summoning a taxi, possibly to catch the return journey of the travelling ice-box.

"Sun hat," said my mother, who was not above squeezing two letters into a single square.

2

Rite of passage: The Welsh passion for funerals

1950s AND 1960s

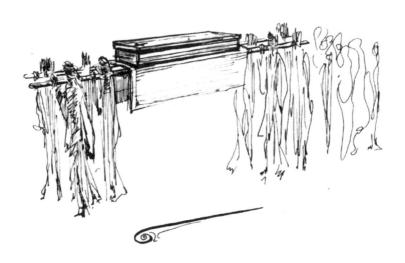

THE PLACE, MERTHYR Tydfil, Wales; the season, winter. I know the last fact because the rain was colder than it is in summer. Each week of our lives was marked by the arrival of the local newspaper, independently-owned then, and full of the recorded doings of worthy people in the neighbourhood. It also told you what was on at the cinema, which is really why most people bought it, and it recorded births, marriages and deaths (hatchings, matchings and despatchings, as they were known locally). It is on this particular part of the newspaper, up toward the front, that we will concentrate for this recollection.

In terms of births, of course, the main characteristic that would stand out if you were to look back at a copy of the paper from the mid 1950s is that there were *a lot of them*. Baby boomers were booming all over Britain, even in Wales, at that time. This required a considerable block of space in the paper, which, happily for the management, brought in a notable amount of revenue. Furthermore, at least according to the announcements, the people actually giving birth to these children were almost all genuinely *married*, though even then quite a few of them had tied the knot ever so slightly *after* the infant had been conceived. Regardless, the event was always portrayed as 'happy', which they probably were for a while.

Marriages were plentiful, and if, again, we were to browse through a yellowed copy of the paper from those days of Doris Day and *The Third Man*, our attention would be caught not so much by the entries, but by the photographs. These couples were *children*, for Heaven's sake. They looked as if they were hardly out of school. Sometimes they weren't, but the modal age of marriage then was about eight to ten years younger than it is now – around 18, and girls matured around 14, not 10 as with growth hormones. Furthermore, there were very few, in fact almost no, *second* marriages unless the entry contained the words 'widow' or 'widower'. Divorce, if it occurred, was *never* mentioned.

And then we come to the part over which we shall linger in truly morbid Welsh fashion: Deaths. The first point to note as we scan the columns is that in those bleaker days, they actually were called that: DEATHS, not Obituaries. They were really *gone*, no two ways about it. The Welsh have a total fascination with departure, in whatever form it manifests itself. So, today, just as it was in the 1950s, when you arrive to stay at the home of a friend or relative, the greeting is always: "Well there's lovely it is to see you, and you are looking so well. When are you going back?"

There is no sinister intent in that last question; it is just that preoccupation with any form of departure – they simply *have* to know. Or there is a need to confirm that a departure really *is* a departure and not something masquerading as goodbye. Hence the conversation I overheard in a pub in Merthyr Vale:

"Did you know that they buried Islwyn Davies last Wednesday?"

"No! Is he dead then?"

Of course, if he were not, then someone is party to a felony. But departure is so important to the Welsh that sometimes it is hard for them to accept that it has really happened. An excellent example was another remark made at the final viewing of a departed soul lying in his box in the living room: "I have never seen him look better."

Before we go on to explore the deaths columns, a word or two about funerals in Wales. First, they were traditionally male-only, though in the modern world that is changing. The woman's role was to stay behind to prepare the food for the return of the mourners. Secondly, you never take the coffin out through the front door. Why? I am not sure, but it was a strong belief which often led to some very complicated manoeuvring, since the back doors of Welsh houses often open into very narrow alleys. Whatever, the exit is hard to achieve with any dignity, and it is also hard not to recall that this is the way the rubbish comes out every Wednesday. There is a terrible symbolism there, but, as far as I know, there is no recorded case of the remains being left for the bin men.

Undertakers, in that era, were generally carpenters, joiners and woodworkers as well as undertakers – and they were called that. Their function was simple: collect, transport and deliver. There were none of the extraordinary doings that Nancy Mitford described in *The American Way of Death*. The American funeral industry was totally incomprehensible to the practical Welsh. As far as they were concerned, great and small all ended up in the same box, which was called a *coffin* and was made of pine. No bronze caskets here. That's it.

The Welsh would always describe a good funeral as a 'nice send-off', though what constituted a *nice* send-off was generally sunshine, a spirited oration, and – most of all – lots of food (and libations) afterwards. Of these, the first factor could not be relied on, and there was no way for people standing around an open hole on a hillside in a downpour to have a 'nice' time, believe me. In fact, it was widely believed in Wales that the premature death of aged or fragile mourners and a quick return to the cemetery, as a customer this time, was a result of standing around in too many 'not-nice' funerals, freezing to death. Undertakers, in particular, hated 'nice' funerals because they slowed down repeat business a lot. They would stand at the edge of the crowd looking hopefully for black clouds and approaching frontal systems over the heads of the frail. Usually they got their way. The more unscrupulous would watch the BBC weather forecast hoping to see a huge low-pressure system sweeping in from the Atlantic. Then they would blame post-war shortages for a delay of a day or two in the coffin.

Back to the newspaper. By the 1950s, the reporting of deaths had, like births and marriages, become totally formulaic. It fell into a four-paragraph module, as follows:

Paragraph 1 would contain, of course, the name, age and address of the deceased, as well as the exact location from which they departed this life. It included a brief summary of their worthy deeds and the fact that they would be 'sorely missed'. Everyone, without exception, was lauded as a perfect parent, pillar of society, etc.

Paragraph 2 consisted of an exhaustive list of all the people who attended the funeral and the nature, if any, of their relationship to the deceased. Since this used up many column inches, this was the *true* indication of how worthy they were. Great care was taken to collect the names and affiliations of everyone who attended the ceremony, or had simply wandered into the cemetery out of curiosity.

Paragraph 3 told you who had made the funeral arrangements, i.e. gave you the undertaker's details.

Paragraph 4 explained where to send flowers, or discussed the deceased's favourite charity, to which tributes should be sent.

In other words, there was not much oratorical or literary content in these announcements and, to be absolutely honest, they all looked the same (huge and boring).

On the occasion we are recounting here, my eye was immediately drawn to an announcement that consisted of *five* paragraphs, which could only mean something unusual and intriguing. You were lured to read it in the same way as Soviets were drawn to join a queue without ever knowing what was at the end of it: if there was a line, there had to be something worth having at the end of it. It was, you might say, an exciting mystery in an otherwise bland existence.

At first glance, the entry seemed normal enough. Of course, I shall not use the real name of the individual. It seemed as though Mr Meirion Williams (82) of Galon Uchaf had passed away. He had the usual list of tributes to his presence on this earth. Then followed the usual list of his family and friends in attendance who had done the job of 'ditching' him, as the Irish used to say, and where to send the tributes.

And then came that aberrant fifth paragraph. It was so extraordinary that it was hard to say whether some cub reporter was making a name by striking out into sensational journalism, or whether, as is more likely, the family wrote up this piece and decided to hand it in with the rest.

What was written is paraphrased here, except for the last line, which no person could ever forget. It ran like this: "During the interment of Mr Williams, one of the mourners at the graveside, Mr Herbert Davies (83), a lifelong friend, slipped in the rain and fell into the open grave. As a result he sustained serious injuries from which he has subsequently died. This tragic event cast a pall of gloom over the whole proceedings."

"A pall of gloom"?

What on earth had they been doing up to that moment – the Hokey Cokey? This is a *funeral*, for Heaven's sake. I understand, of course, that it must have been a dramatic shock even on that bleak, windswept, rain-sodden hillside, and a terrible blow to everyone except the undertaker, who probably never in his life had anticipated this rapid a turnround in business. Perhaps he thought about ways to start up assembly-line burials. I am certain that he quietly inspected the edge of the grave afterwards to see if there was some sort of creative mining work he could do in future to encourage a reappearance of the 'pall of gloom' on a somewhat regular basis.

Sure enough, Mr Davies' demise was there in print the next Friday, but was only allocated the regular four paragraphs. His glory had been stolen by lifelong friend Meirion. Tough break.

Follow that hearse

Staying on this subject, I was personally involved in only one 'real' funeral, and that was quite enough for me. At the time I had taken a summer job, driving for an elderly couple who lived close to my home. They had a car, but neither of them drove, so why they had the car I do not know. Anyway, they asked me to drive for them and I agreed. The problem, as it turned out, was that they never went anywhere, or if they did, they walked.

That is until *his* father died. The deceased gentleman had been in a retirement home (or Old Folks' Home, as it was more prosaically called then) on the other side of town. He had been laid out down there, and the funeral procession would proceed from the home to the cemetery. At the last moment, I received the call to drive them to the home, and then follow the hearse with them to the burial.

I rushed up to their house only to find that the large, black car had a flat battery. There was not an ounce of juice in it.

This was a consequence of their never using their car. I told them to take a taxi, and meanwhile, I said optimistically that with some assistance I would move the car out onto the hill and jump-start it. So off they went, leaving me to work out how to get the car out of the garage, which backed *up* into a lane that opened onto the steep hill of the main road.

I could make no impression on this elephantine automobile, and when I put my back against the radiator and pushed with all my might, my feet went through the back of the garage. My bacon was saved by the arrival of the milkman. No, that is not strictly true: it was his horse that saved the day. The milkman unhitched the nag and after attaching a towrope, managed to haul the car backwards out onto the main road facing downhill. After releasing the one-horse power car from its power source, I hopped in, and mercifully, the car jump-started and we were on our way.

I drove to the retirement home as fast as I dared, arriving there to find that there were no vehicles parked in the visitor car park. This was ominous. I dashed in and asked the receptionist:

"Have you seen a funeral?"

"I've seen all too many. My Aunt Gwen passed away last..."

"No, I mean here, now – a funeral leaving???"

"Right. Yes, they went some minutes ago but they can't have gone too far, you know, because – well, they don't exactly race," she wisely observed.

Of course, that was it. So I dashed for the car, crossed my fingers and turned the key. It started, and knowing in what direction they were headed, I tore off in pursuit of the remains. It seems they were doing more of a foxtrot than a funeral march in that hearse because I couldn't catch up with them. I became reckless, passing cars whenever the slightest opportunity offered itself in order to catch up to the back of the cortege. Then I got stuck behind a line of cars. I was weaving in and out looking for a chance to pass them.

Finally it came. Shifting down a gear, I squeezed every ounce of energy out of the venerable vehicle. Just as I was about to clear the entire line, I noticed that the first vehicle was a hearse. There was nothing I could do, of course, because I had committed myself to pass. The elderly couple saw me, smiled and waved as I shot by. They must have wondered what on earth I was doing, but at least they were reassured to see that I had made it.

Now I was *leading* the funeral. That was not good, so I pulled off to a side street, where I thought I could turn around and then neatly fall in behind the cortege. Too late, I realised that the street was too narrow to let me turn this old monster of a car around. Now I was committed to drive on until I could go around three sides of what I hoped would be a square. Well, whatever it was I turned into, it never added up to a square and, instead. I found myself driving off perpendicular to the route of the funeral. All this took time, and of course, and the funeral procession was long gone by the time I was finally headed in the right direction. It was at that point that I realised I did not know towards *which of the two cemeteries* at this end of town they were heading. That was because they had never told me, never imagining that I would end up going there on my own.

I took a chance and chose one. When I pulled up at the gate, a very elderly sexton was standing there with a wheelbarrow. I leapt from the car and rushed up to him:

"Excuse me, I'm looking for a funeral…" I exclaimed.

"You have definitely come to the right place," he observed slowly, removing his pipe.

"No, I mean now – do you have one?"

"Totally out boyo, try again tomorrow."

"Damn."

This meant that I would have to hightail it over to the *other* cemetery, which I did, but now the rush hour was on, and you know how it is: the greater the need for speed, the more likely it is that a learner driver in an old truck has decided to have his first lesson.

The upshot? When I got there, it was all over, and the mourners were coming out of the gate. The sun was shining so, I was told, he had had a 'nice send off'. The undertaker was angrily looking up at the blue sky, presumably thinking, "I hate summer. Bring on the winter when they die like flies."

My charges were the last to leave, and I stood there with the door open. "Brave lad," he said. "You missed a nice send-off."

"Yes, it was lovely," echoed his wife. No pall of gloom there, thank Heavens.

3

Cars for concern: Hiding one's light under the boot

WALES, 1950s

MY FATHER'S LIFE revolved around cars professionally, recreationally and, for a while in the 1930s, competitively. My mother, on the other hand, entertained no mechanical knowledge whatsoever. This dichotomy had the potential for some rather serious differences of opinion in which science did not always triumph over intuition.

Our annual holiday in the late 1940s and early 1950s was always spent in Tenby, a coastal resort in Pembrokeshire. It was, and is, for me a magical place, with its tall turn-of-the-century hotels crenellating the clifftop that curves round to encompass a splendid bay. At that age, I thought that this must be New York, so tall and majestic were the hotels. Even if it *had* been New York, I could not have loved it more, for it spelled out sand, sea, and possibly sun too, as well as ice-creams, old castles and the thrill of a place that existed only for holidays. I recall that the cry of a seagull was the first indication we were entering the zone of enchantment. I would lie in bed in our lodging house during the first night listening to the avian fanfare of the kingdom of vacations. But first, of course, we had to get there.

Packing the car was never a chore for me because (a) I didn't do it, and (b) we were taking all the fun things for digging sand, catching fish and so on. I never divined my parents' feelings about it, but after the privations of wartime, and with money still very tight, holidays were *special*, like strawberries, chicken and other things that have become totally commonplace now. The journey lay through the treeless majesty of the Brecon Beacons, along whose deeply glaciated valleys and past whose majestic lakes we motored on the first leg.

Then there was a turn, like a secret door, which took us out of the main valley and up along a wooded road, occasionally the width of one car. But this was *the* turn that truly signalled leaving the land of work and routine for *the sea*. Holidays were not confirmed until that straight horizon of blue was glimpsed, the quality of the air began to change, and, of course, the chance that one of those seagulls might shriek a welcome. But, that vision was still hours away. First we had to meander through sheep country and sleepy towns, anxious to count off the markers that we looked for each time: the triangular stone that commemorated the point at which a stagecoach had left the road and plunged into the valley bringing death to all; the sharp right-hand bend where, a year or so before, a car had met the same fate; Merlin's Oak in Carmarthen, where the desiccated remains of a tree stood, incongruously, on the pavement, enchanted by Merlin so that when it fell, the town would go with it;[5] and the house in the same town where, at some distant point, the child of the household had graced the advertisements for Pear's Soap.

So far we have journeyed through an ideal form of the excursion, but there was one thing that could change all that, and often did. That thing was rain. Wales is one of the wettest places in Great Britain, and the epitome of crashing boredom was always represented by the phrase 'like a wet, Welsh Sunday'. In wet weather you kept the car windows shut (smokers notwithstanding), which invariably resulted in my feeling sick. In addition, there was the awful prospect of a washed-out holiday, plus we would take much longer to spot the sea and we could well duplicate the fate of that stagecoach. The particular day I have in mind, it *poured*.

All went well for most of the journey, though the mood was definitely low-key. Then, just beyond Carmarthen, the car's engine started to falter as though there was water in the petrol. It jumped and jerked and eventually stopped as my father cruised into a lay-by. He donned his mackintosh and trilby and braved his way out of the car, gaining some meagre shelter under its huge, lifted bonnet. There he began a fiddling and tweaking; that much my mother and I made out through the steamed-up windows of the car. In rain, in those days, no matter what you did, the car steamed up totally like a mobile sauna. Someone was then delegated to wipe the driver's side regularly with a cloth. Furthermore, this 'sitting it out' posture was not that unfamiliar to my mother and me, since punctures were common then and wheel changes were all part of the daily round of driving.

Eventually, my father slammed the bonnet, rushed back into the car and turned the key. There was a whisper of response but that quickly died, leaving us back just where we had been. This, of course, meant another journey into the monsoon for

---

5   The last remains of the tree were actually removed in 1978, so Carmarthen is presumably on borrowed time.

my father, and he had just cracked open the door when my mother said from the passenger seat: "Val, I don't know if this is important, but I noticed that the light wasn't working in the boot when we were loading. Could that have something to do with it?"

My father was a patient man, and a gentleman too, so he said, "There is no connection between the illumination of the boot and the ignition system, so thank you for the idea but I will go back and see if I can sort the engine out."

My mother smiled a knowing smile, though we never had the remotest idea what she thought she knew at those times.

By now the rain had turned into a maelstrom, and my father meanwhile was doing something active with a spanner. We could hear the reverberations from inside, Then, steaming slightly, he came running back inside. Turn the key once more, look of concentration, prayer and frustration; some ignition, almost a sustained start, followed by – *nothing*. My father's patience was being sorely tested, especially as he was 'Mr Car', and it was inconceivable that an internal combustion engine could outwit him. He was deep in thought and steam when my mother, still staring through the windscreen, remarked, "You know, they're both electrical things. There *could* be a connection. Why don't you at least have a look?"

The gentleman in him won, and he said that, yes, he would have a look in the boot and see if, by chance, some part of the ignition system had wandered around the car and hidden in there. He gave a sigh and went, teeth clenched, through the tempest and round to the back of the car. By now he took little care to stay dry because he was thoroughly saturated. We heard the boot lid open, some minor shaking of the car took place, and then he came back inside. Battered, but not quite defeated, he said: "Happy now? Somehow the bulb had worked loose and was not making a good connection. I tightened it, and it is working perfectly once again. Would you like me to get inside and close the lid to make sure it goes off when you close it, like the fridge?"

"No, I believe you; but why don't you, at least, try the engine now that the bulb is firmly tightened up?" my mother enquired, since making us mobile again had been the purpose of her suggestion in the first place.

My father took a deep breath but, very commendably, kept his thoughts to himself. He turned the key, and the engine roared into life. He stared through the windshield as though he had been hit with a wet mackerel. My mother, of course, said absolutely nothing, which is a hundred times more effective than "*see, I told you to try it...*" She simply folded her hands in her lap and, looking to the heavens, said, "Aha! I see a patch of blue over there big enough to mend a sailor's trousers, so we will probably arrive there in the sunshine."

My father did not respond, and indeed, kept his own counsel for the rest of the rain-soaked journey, until it ended with us entering Tenby to the accompaniment of a glorious sunny summer evening.

The driving lesson

Even though my father and cars were inseparable, my mother did not drive. This was despite her holding a provisional driving licence for over twenty years – and I believe she died in this unfulfilled condition. Since everyone in the family, my infant self excepted, had a car, there was hardly any need for her to drive. Furthermore, her mother owned a general store that was next door and her brother worked there and had a car. Also nearby was the bus stop. There was, however, evidence that she *had* driven, and that took the form of a photograph of her in Cardiganshire at the wheel of an open tourer along with eleven children. I was assured by 'Uncle Reg' (the man to whom Timothy Evans surrendered himself on November 30th

1949[6]) that, subsequent to the picture being taken, my mother drove them all into a haystack in the middle of the field.

"I don't think she had it in mind to do that," he said, in suitably law-officer terms.

However, one day, for some reason I no longer remember, something happened that motivated her to drive (again?). Maybe my father had to be away on business, or was temporarily immobilised, or temporarily lost his mind, but that really does not matter. What does matter was that my mother was, once more, behind the wheel of a car. I confess, immediately, that I never witnessed this in all the years she and I were alive at the same time. But, it did happen.

Fearing an almost certain emergence of irreconcilable marital differences if my father were to be her instructor, they talked my brother (ten years my senior) into taking her out. My father took a very philosophical view of the whole thing, and used to discuss the concept of the internal combustion engine and the symbiotic relationship between man and machine. Here I will digress. He had, over the previous decade, developed a deepening affection for ever-more titanic vehicles imported from the United States, which were wholly unsuited to what passed for roads in Wales at that time. Indeed, when I measured one of them, it was longer than the front of our modest terraced house. He lived and breathed those cars, and Sunday was devoted to a full hand wash and wax polish. The more gadgets these cars had, the better he admired them. One of them, a Ford Galaxy 500 Convertible in an unbelievable

---

6   In British legal history, Timothy Evans looms large. His wife and unborn child may or may not have been victims of the mass murderer Reginald Christie, who disposed of his eight (or ten) victims in the framework of his house and in the garden. Though Evans was executed, he was subsequently pardoned (a dubious privilege), but the arguments rage to this day about whether or not he committed the murder of his own family. 'Uncle' Inspector Reg Wilson was the policeman to whom Evans surrendered. That was not the end of his problems, for he was also the senior police officer handling the dreadful disaster of Aberfan, where the long-predicted collapse of a badly-located slag heap wiped out an entire generation of schoolchildren.

bronze colour, looking like a mobile ingot, had an automatic roof that opened and closed on command. It was my poor mother's fate one Sunday, returning from a visit to a relative on the English border, to be passing through Newport, Monmouthshire, in heavy rain (again). While waiting at some town-centre traffic lights, my father began fiddling with the clamps that held the top firmly down in the closed position. Then, in the middle of his task, the lights changed, and the car behind started honking for him to go. He became flustered, pulled away quickly and must have inadvertently pressed the critical button that activated the roof. It is very strange to follow a car whose roof suddenly folds itself away into the boot as it is moving. It is even more extraordinary to encounter this spectacle during a deluge. My mother said not a word. Instead, she quickly raised her umbrella, looking for all the world like the Queen Mother braving the elements.

But to return to the driving lesson. My mother had gone out in my father's monster vehicle with my brother. Before too long they were back, whereupon she entered the room where my father and I were sitting and threw the keys on the table, saying, "Right. That's it! I am not driving any more. In fact, I *hate* driving."

My father took the philosophical road:

"Now, you are being emotional and irrational. You can't say '*I hate driving*'. People like you drive every day, and they don't get into a state. You always enjoy a ride in the car, so let's see what is really the problem. What *exactly* is it you 'hate' about driving? Be specific."

"Everything. It's not for me."

To which my father sagely shook his head, and went on: "Now, let's analyse this. Ask yourself what it is about driving that you don't like. Then we can concentrate on that and straighten it out. OK?"

My mother, who had by now calmed down a little, nodded and said: "Parking. I hate parking."

My father nodded like Oliver Hardy after proving a point to

Stan, wagged his index finger and proceeded: "You see, now we are getting somewhere. Right, let's focus down a little more. What *exactly* is it about parking that you do not like?"

My mother looked thoughtful for a moment, and then said: "That horrible scraping noise."

My father was fast going into shock, but lived long enough to leap from his seat and out through the door to where he knew the car, or what was left of it, was parked. My mother watched him go and said: "He must have remembered something, he doesn't usually get up that fast. Have you had tea yet?"

A question of colour

We have already encountered my father's short-term memory problem, and sometimes it would manifest itself in wonderfully unexpected ways. On occasion he came home to join my mother, brother and me for lunch. During the course of one particularly memorable meal he looked up and, using a fork for emphasis, remarked to my brother:

"I had the devil's own time trying to start the car today, which is why I am a bit late. It may be that there is something loose in the ignition-key socket, or it is very worn. Anyway, I have not noticed it before, so do you mind taking a look at it while I finish my lunch?"

My brother, who had already finished his lunch and was into the newspaper, reached out for the keys. My mother said to him, "Now, don't be long, because we have arctic roll today."

My brother was quickly out of the door, and even more rapidly back again. My mother looked pleased and a slice of arctic roll swiftly rewarded his velocity.

My father, who had just settled into his newspaper, was surprised and baffled by the speed with which his son had dealt with something that had bettered Mr Car and made him late. Of course, he had to ask, "Well, did you sort out the problem? It foxed me."

My brother looked at him and said, "It was easy. The colour was wrong."

My father was clearly baffled, and it took a lot to baffle him. Eventually he said inquisitively, "What has the colour of the ignition – and I didn't know they had a colour – got to do with anything? You mean *the colour of the wires?*"

My brother looked at my mother as he answered because he knew she was going to love this one.

"The ignition, in fact, has nothing to do with it. It is more to do with the colour of the car. Yes, I would say 100%, that's it."

My father was truly confused now and looked from my brother to my mother and back. My mother sensed something was up, but was as much at sea as my father.

"I have no idea what you are talking about – *the colour of the car?*"

"Yes. You see your car is black, and this car, similar though it is, is dark green. By some miracle, with enough force you can just about get the key into the slot and start it. However, I would try to remember where you got into it, and park it back there as soon as possible. The authorities are probably looking for it."

My father made one of his now familiar hasty exits and drove off quickly toward town.

"How is the arctic roll today?" my mother enquired. "The right colour, I hope?"

4

Coming out of the closet, or The Dutch lieutenant's jacket

THE NETHERLANDS AND CREWE JUNCTION, 1964

IN SPRING A young man's fancy lightly turns to wondering why if, in 1937, the average American male owned only three changes of clothes, today I can't get near – never mind walk into – my wardrobe. Far down the dark end near the entrance to Narnia, I found several items that had not been worn since the Great Society came and went. Among these was, long forgotten, the uniform of a lieutenant in the Royal Dutch East Indies Marines. You have all experienced the 'clearing out' phenomenon. It ends up with you, surrounded by more chaos than you thought possible, looking at Uncle Wilfred in the Nash Tourer picnicking somewhere in the Great Plains. The uniform was the beginning and end of the effort for me. I decided to commit it to the miracle of eBay, and as I write, it is sailing to Sydney, Australia. My only regret is that its new owner will never know the extraordinary provenance of that unlikely garment.

The year was 1963; the venue, the Netherlands, where I had just arrived in the rain and darkness to begin a geological field trip with my Cola-addicted colleague Dave Clark (no, not the one with the band). I had my simple needs accommodated in a modest suitcase, which at that moment was residing by my left foot in the tram. We had just disembarked from the crossing of the North Sea – for Britain was unequivocally an island in those days – to the Hook of Holland. Neither of us was totally compos mentis after that experience, especially as we tried to accommodate the jerky progress of the tram, when we had only just found our sea legs for the long swell.

When we came to our tram stop, I reached down, only to find a case-less void. It had gone. Really in no condition for this situation, we reported it to the police, but that still left me without anything other than what I was wearing, which was not going to last the duration. And money was tight, even though Prime Minister McMillan had told me, just that very month, that "I had never had it so good".

The immediate problem was to get kitted out for the field with something durable and cheap. Some Dutch friends told me to try the flea market, which would be up and running in the morning – even if we wouldn't be. So, the following morning found Dave and me picking among the mountains of unlikely things, but finding nothing suitable in my price range. At that point, Dave leaned over and said, "There's always *this*," holding up an olive-green jacket of fine tailoring. The only difficulty I could divine was that it was strewn with lanyards, epaulettes, stars and the like. "But," he said, "it is only £3 for the lot, and it looks new." It certainly had copious pockets (much loved

41

by geologists for errant fossils, hammers and the like), and I found that it fitted admirably.

"But I can't walk around in this," I said.

"Sure you can," the tallholder said, flourishing his cigarette.

There was not really time for much discourse as we had to be back at the hostel to meet up with the rest of the party and depart for strata unknown. So I bought it.

In fact, the uniform served me well, and everyone got used to it after the initial shock. Remember, this was when The Beatles were posing on their *Sergeant Pepper* album cover looking like refugees from the Ruritanian Royal Guard. But the purchase did not begin to work its magic until we were on our way home. In fact, by then I had become so used to wearing the outfit, I had forgotten I was masquerading as a Marine. I even knew what rank and unit I represented because I found a love letter in the pocket addressed to a Marine in the Netherlands East Indies (which packed up and went away round about 1949, so that dated the coat).

It is every British person's fate to be changing trains at Crewe station at 1 a.m. at some point in their life. It is our equivalent of Warhol's '15 minutes of fame'. On this occasion it was to be shared with the dour Mr Clark. We had arrived from the coast, and were seeking food at this bleak transit point. The railway buffet was still open, and so we made our way toward the light. I was not to know, of course, that our arrival in Crewe was, as they would say now, coterminous with the end of a NATO exercise, and so I happened to walk into the smoke-choked buffet to find an entire company of Dutch soldiers waiting for a connection to go the way we had just come. I thought nothing of it, until they all stood up. I could not imagine what was happening until Dave said "Salute them, *now*." I did, and they sat down, and we hastened behind the protection of a container of sausage rolls.

After we had made a discreet exit, I said, "I don't think I want to stand around on the platform in this outfit saluting, so let's find our train."

"But there is over an hour before it leaves," Dave observed.

"We can sleep," I reminded him. And so we made our way to the darkened train, itself snoozing before its rush into central Wales.

Being students, we never did the logical and obvious, and so I opened the door to the *only* compartment that had the window blinds drawn. You have all seen this in the movies, and I am here to tell you it actually happens. As I slid the door aside, a body slowly fell on top of me. Dave said, once the unidentified dead weight and I had hit the floor together, "Is he still breathing?" The recumbent victim had certainly been roughed up in a heavy-duty manner.

"How am I supposed to know that?" I spluttered. "I can hardly breathe myself with this weight on top of me."

Dave rolled the fellow aside, and suggested we had better get the Transport Police. He did just that, and a railway constable (whom Dave, for reasons known only to himself, always addressed as *Constabule*), came in, and declared the victim unconscious but still of this world. Then, as police are wont to do, he asked what had happened. There was almost nothing we could tell him. He took down the usual details, never once asking why I was dressed in the uniform of a foreign power. However, I think his instinctive respect for the uniformed forces, wherever they originated, helped clear me of involvement. Plus, the place was awash with people in uniform anyway. The situation was helped enormously by the eventual return from Planet Mongo of the now-recovered victim, who then totally exonerated us.

That over, we entered the mysterious compartment, which by now had been occupied by an elderly couple. During the course of the subsequent journey, they too never asked me my name, rank or serial number. But the gentleman did keep looking at me in a very odd and persistent way.

"This isn't really my uniform," I volunteered, thinking that was the source of his bemusement.

"Oh no," he said, "I'm sorry, it wasn't that. It's just that you look so much like someone I remember from long ago. In fact, it's quite frightening because he was not the sort of person you would ever want to cross. Indeed no. But I did, and he called round to my house, and laid me out with a tyre lever."

"Indeed," I commented, "and when was this?"

"Oh, my word, now you're asking. It's got to be around the First World War – wasn't it?" he said, turning to his wife.

Well," she offered, "I know it was back when we lived in Dixon Street, dear."

Now they *really* had my attention because *my grandfather*, a man of means and memorably demonstrative emotions, had *also* lived in Dixon Street.

"Strange seeing you like that. Brought it all back," the elderly gentleman went on.

My grandfather became the fatal victim of a secret drinker who was also his chauffeur in 1929, almost twenty years before I entered the drama of life. He was killed returning from a night of triumph after his son, my uncle, won the British 'Golden Helmet' for dirt-track motorcycle racing.

"What was his name again?" mused the old fellow, and, as is so often the case, his wife did not hesitate to fish the information from the depths.

"Harry Baker," she said.

"Hey," said Dave, uncharacteristically alert, "Didn't you tell me – ?"

His line of thought was interrupted when a Dutch military size eleven shoe accidentally disengaged several of his toes.

"How extraordinary," I said, moving on quickly to the weather.

That, I suppose, should have been that. But it wasn't. Five *years* later, I received a notification from Customs that a package had arrived for me from foreign parts. I could not imagine what it could be. It was my suitcase, which had started the whole affair. It still contained all the contents that had departed with it from the tram that night.

"Why did I need the customs inspection?" I asked the officer when I collected it.

"Because of where it originated," he replied.

"The Netherlands," I responded, confused.

"No, sir, it came from Rostock in East Germany," he said, with a sinister slow rendering of the name *East Germany*. It was, I thought, a wonderfully apt, quite inexplicable, and suitably bizarre ending to the long-forgotten tale of the Dutch Marine's uniform. Watch out for strange happenings in the Sydney area around about two months from now. The eBay consignment should be pulling in right about then.

5

Fighting unemployment in rural Norfolk

ENGLAND, 1973

THE DAY HAD started normally enough: there were no unpromising signs, omens, portents or problems. Indeed it bode well to be a good example of what Henry James so truly declared:

> Summer afternoon, summer afternoon, to me those have always been the two most evocative words in the English language.

In total compliance with his sentiments, a brilliant July sun stood brazen and high in the sky. Who, I thought, could fail to be enthused by the transcendent bucolic charm of the rays blinking randomly among the broad leaves gently stirring in the languid breeze; well, *something like that*. Turning from the vantage point at the open kitchen door, I saw my wife at the sink, looking deep in thought, and clearly moved as was I. Taking in all this loveliness, and doubtless searching for the *mot juste*, she remarked: "Why do you think the hot water is dark brown?"

It took a while for me to connect the prosaic observation on plumbing with the reincarnation of John Constable's landscape around me, but I realised she was speaking from the planet Here-and-Now – Station Down-to-Earth.

"The hot water is dark brown? Did you have it turned off for a long time, like three months?"

"No," she replied with one of those grudging sighs, "Remember, we washed the dishes right here in this very spot less than 24 hours ago."

"Ah, yes, you're right" I admitted quickly, now fully engaged; like all men, praying it would sort itself out without the intervention of my labour or our bank account. "Still continuing to run brown, is it?" I enquired, but knowing full well that these things never sort themselves out.

"I can't tell," she replied enigmatically.

"How is it possible that you cannot tell the colour of the water?" I enquired, puzzled.

"Because the water has stopped altogether and could now be any colour, *wherever it has gone*. However, there *is* a new and ominous rumbling noise," she observed with an ear on the tap.

I hurried upstairs to one of the bedrooms in our old and modest red-brick farmhouse, where dwelt the immersion heater. In those days, anyway, it was very difficult to tell anything by standing there and simply looking at a water heater, since there were no diagnostic dials or warnings. It

47

looked the same as it always did: a totally inert copper tank, which was not producing hot water but was producing a deep rumbling and tortured metal sound. This was clearly a case for a plumber.

At this point one complication needs to be mentioned. That very day, in that selfsame bedroom, Arthur – of solid East Anglian stock[7] – was, at a pace in keeping with the torpor of the day, putting up wallpaper. I will make an attempt here to recreate his almost impenetrable Norfolk dialect, because it had, since time immemorial, put the locals on a different wavelength. Nonetheless, I was beginning to decipher the local patois now.

"Have you gotta problem then?" he asked, as I used the layman's method of fixing things by banging them hard with my fist.

"Yep. Hot water is a gonner. Don't know what's wrong," I explained after fully analysing the results of the beating the heater had just taken from me.

Arthur then informed me as, atop his ladder, he regarded me over his shoulder. "Ah now, that's interesting because I'm a-getting' round that way and will be working on that cupboard there soon as can be."

The cupboard in question, of course, was the one that housed the water heater that had just passed away, snugly, in its space. I could see Arthur's point because, if the plumber came over, Arthur could not wallpaper in the same space as his fellow tradesman was plumbing. So, in conclusion, Arthur informed me, "No doubt you're a-gonna call for a plumber, and I wish you good luck with that. But if you don't mind, I will sit this out on my trestle a-here and await further news and developments."

---

7   Norfolk, despite being so close to London, was out on a geographical limb, and tended to get passed by. The local people called people from outside *strangers*, but if their parents or grandparents, or indeed any identifiable ancestor, were known to *have moved* here, they were referred to as *local* strangers.

With that he abandoned any pretence at the wallpapering, descended the ladder, sat down on the trestle, and with a contented sigh, opened a copy of the *Daily Mirror*. Right. I hastened away to make a phone call. To provide you with same sort of historical context, I can tell you that in those days our phone number was Drayton 174, and we were still all excited about rotary dialling.

In the United Kingdom, obtaining the services of a plumber within the same geological epoch is usually an uphill task and I needed one straight away, otherwise I was paying Arthur to update himself on current affairs. So, with little anticipation of success, I called, and hit gold on the first attempt. He would be "round in a flash". And he was. His name was Godfrey and he was of approximately the same vintage as Arthur. After he had bulleted down our gravel drive between the privet hedges at an impressive speed, he fairly leapt from the van, hand outstretched.

"Now then," he said, shaking hands and looking set for business, "where is the tank?"

I led him upstairs, where he was surprised to see Arthur, his legs swinging, and by now deep in the sports section.

"How's it going there?" Arthur said. "Don't mind me, but I can't proceed until you've a-had a look at the old tank there. Could be all sorts of *implications*."

"Right," said Godfrey. "I'm on top of it."

"You'd a-better be careful not to fall off then," chuckled Arthur, shaking his head in a previously unheralded display of wit.

Godfrey opened his copious tool bag, enquired where the stopcock was located, and went to turn off the water about half a mile away beyond the end of the lawn and into the trees, where wise people do not venture to go. When he came back in and went upstairs, the wife asked where he'd been.

"Oh, to turn off the water," I replied.

"What water?" she said, studying the back lawn through the kitchen window.

Upstairs, he then set to work examining the patient. I returned to my position in the kitchen, but it was only a matter of minutes before Godfrey came downstairs and mournfully announced: "It's shot; a total goner, and I am going to have to replace it."

I groaned because now we were not only facing unanticipated expenses, but also, who knows what length of delay? With a vague foreboding that I would have to start lending Arthur books, I nervously enquired as to the consequences of this diagnosis.

"Oh, don't worry, it is not as bad as it sounds. We just whip that one out, plumb in a new one and Bob's your uncle. But first, I have to find a replacement and that heater is not a spring chicken."

The God of Telephones was with us that day, for Godfrey found what he needed right away and it was just up the road.

"I'm away to get the heater. Once I'm back it should take me no time," he assured us with a cheery wave and off he went in the van.

He was back in a remarkably short space of time, during which I kept up Arthur's spirits with a cup of tea. He was very philosophical about the whole thing. Arthur even left his literary perch to help Godfrey as soon as the van returned. They struggled up the stairs with the gleaming new tank, and it did indeed look like a souped-up twentieth-century version of the old one.

"Righty-ho," exclaimed Godfrey, rotating his shoulders and looking earnest, "I'll turn the electricity off and get to it right away, but first of all I need to drain your old immersion heater, otherwise even the old team here will never be able to lift it. I'll need to run this hosepipe out the window," which he proceeded to do.

As a torrent of rusty water cascaded out of our bedroom window, Godfrey joined Arthur in a cup of tea and a section of the *Mirror*.

"Very restful, that is," said Arthur.

"What is?" Godfrey enquired.

"The sound of flowing water. On a day like this, fairly makes you want to have a picnic, like," Arthur responded, carried away by the romance of it all.

Eventually, once the area around the front door was flooded, the flow ceased and Godfrey declared himself ready to switch immersion heaters.

"I'll get out of your way," I remarked.

"Yes, and as soon as I am done, I'll come down and tell you. We can test the flow and then I can explain anything you need to know," he said in a businesslike manner, gripping a big spanner.

"I'll just pop off and make you some tea, then," I volunteered, wanting to feel as though I had some part.

"I'd love that," Godfrey responded, "though I'm not entirely sure how, without any water in the house."

"Ah, yes," I acknowledged, beaten again, and slowly closed the door and returned to the kitchen. "This is tremendously efficient and impressive. Never thought we would find a plumber that fast!" I remarked to my wife.

However, even my wonderment at the speed of things was not prepared for the speed with which Godfrey actually appeared in the kitchen. On the other hand, his brow was knitted in concern.

"Wrong sort of tank?" I enquired.

"No, tank's fine. Perfect. But I need to ask you if *you* put the old tank in."

"Oh, no, that was long before my time," I told him, since the tank had come with the house.

His concern deepened and I could not imagine what the problem could be, but of course, I was about to find out.

"The problem is not with the tank, it's with the cupboard it's in. You see, my belief is that the cupboard was built *after* the tank was installed."

"How on earth would you know that?" I asked, genuinely puzzled.

51

"Well," came the answer, "the tank is wider than the doorframe, and so it, for certain, weren't put in there after the cupboard was constructed."

I was not sure where we were going with this one, but supposed I had to know. "What *does that mean*? What will you have to do?" I asked.

"Me, nothing," he responded, "but that cupboard door frame is gonna have to come off before I can install your immersion heater. But *that*," he said with some determination, "is a job for a carpenter. I don't even have the tools for that kind of work."

With a sinking feeling, I asked Godfrey if he knew of a carpenter who would come at short notice. With a sharp intake of a breath that always accompanies the response to a ridiculous question he suggested the name of someone he had "used before". He called him and, wonder of wonders, the fellow said he would be right around. Fortunately, Arthur's trestle was wide enough for two, so Godfrey joined him while we awaited the arrival of our third craftsman of the day.

His name was John and he was younger than the other two. However, he seemed very convivial and so, was rapidly accepted into the tradesmen's commune forming in my bedroom. The situation was quickly explained, with Arthur chiming in with what a good thing it was that he had not started papering in that corner. John reassured us that there was no serious structural work, as the whole cupboard was what he graphically termed "a flimsy afterthought". I left him tearing it to pieces and went back to the kitchen.

The next arrival came spontaneously and was totally unknown to me, as was the name on his large truck. He had come on that day quite coincidentally, as a result of a long-forgotten transaction we had set up. This time, from the big truck came a short man in a flat cap, who approached the kitchen door.

"I've come," he said, "Sorry it took so long. Oh, is that tea?"[8]

"Why of course, I'm sorry, do come and join us," I welcomed him, before venturing to ask the key question: "Excuse me, it's awfully silly, but I can't remember what you were going to do," I said, looking discomfited.

"The barn, sir. *The barn*, that's what it's all about." He said this in a sort of Sam Weller way.

At that point I remembered exactly who he was. We had a barn at the bottom of our yard that was in impending danger of collapse. I had asked around for someone who could take it down and haul it off. And, by George, four months later, here he was.

"Oh, of course, I totally forgot! I thank you for coming," I said.

"Not at all, sir. Not at all. No problem there. But, if you don't mind me asking, I see all them other vans. Have I come at a difficult time?"

"No, the others are all in the bedroom. They won't get in your way," I told him. "Feel free to carry on."

"I would," he said apologetically, "but them vans is between my truck and the barn." It took a sort of vehicular chess to resolve this, but eventually the truck drove down to the barn.

This whole day was turning into a circus, but was still within manageable proportions with only four trade guilds represented, though I was worried how many more people would join Arthur on the trestle and what the capacity of the sturdy wooden horse really was. I was ready for another cup of tea, but now the water was really gone. But something stronger would probably be efficacious now.

The sherry was, in fact, about halfway down my throat when there was a mighty bang.

---

8 Confused? Was Godfrey's earlier observation somehow wrong? No. My wife had been in the process of preparing to boil vegetables before the water and power had been turned off, and thus had a large saucepan filled with water into which not one vegetable had yet ventured.

"What the hell was that? Where did it come from?" I asked my wife, who was still standing at the sink, watching progress on the barn through the window. "It sounded like it came from the barn," I ventured.

"What barn?" she replied, looking out of the kitchen window.

Almost immediately the 'barn man', whose name I still did not know at this point, was at the door.

"Are you all right?" I enquired, wondering if the bang had been part of something intentional or not.

"What? Oh, me – yes, I'm fine. We just decided to help it on its way with a rope and the truck. But," (Here was the word I was beginning to dread. *But*.) "that barn does not have an earth floor as you thought it had and as you *told* us it had. We found that under the earth is a foot of solid concrete and the uprights are set into that. Damn thing well-nigh pulled the back off the truck. So it is only half down. The concrete has to go."

I agreed wholeheartedly, not really understanding what on earth he was talking about, or what had really caused the bang. It was simply his truck morphing into a new shape.

"Go right ahead," I assured him, decisively.

"There ain't no way I can raise that concrete – that requires someone with a compressor and pneumatic jacks."

Aha, I thought. This whole thing is beginning to fall into a pattern. So, without really needing to, I posed the following question: "Whom do we call?"

"Ah, well now, sir – that's an easy one. This village of Drayton contains one of the largest contractors in the area and if Mr Carter don't have a compressor, I shall be a very surprised man, very surprised. Do you mind if I use the phone?"

I assured him that the phone was available and working, as had been proven many times that afternoon. Once more he was totally successful and told me that the compressor was on its way, along with "not one, sir, but two" men with jackhammers. Given the proximity of the company, they were pulling in almost as soon as the phone was down.

You may find it hard to remember, but this tale began with

reflections on a torrid summer day at peace with the world. OK, you can cancel the Wordsworth and think Fritz Lang. From above came the sound of walls being ripped out, but that was barely audible above the racket of World War III coming from the unanticipated concrete slab. It was no wonder we did not catch the modest tintinnabulation of the doorbell.

It was the postman with a registered letter. Getting no response, he wandered around the side. Standing there in bewilderment, he looked around at the vans and trucks, and remarked, "You are well on your way to becoming the largest employer of tradesmen in the county, sir. We all owe you a debt of gratitude. What are you doing that requires a decorator, a plumber, a carpenter, a contractor and a demolition company? Even when they do build a new house, it's a rare day they are all there together." He scratched his forehead under the peak of his Post Office hat.

I told him that I agreed with him, and the next letter he would be delivering would be the notice of bankruptcy proceedings.

"Hello Arthur," the postman shouted, for Arthur had finished the paper many times over and was leaning out of the window watching the cricket match on the village field opposite. "What are you doing?"

"Right now, bugger all," said Arthur. "I'm third in line behind the plumber and the joiner."

The postman paused for a moment, looked up at Arthur, who was disputing a catch by the opposing team on the Green, and said, "Arthur, I tell you what bothers me."

"What's that, Grenville?" he asked, without turning his head.

"You are lacking only an electrician, and you know my brother Grill is an electrician. Should I give him the nod?" he continued.

"No, nothing electrical – definitely nothing electrical," I intervened, hastily. "But I will keep him in mind if we get struck by lightning. Now let me sign for the letter, and then you can deliver all your foreclosure, divorce, and final demand notices."

For those of you wondering where the registered letter is going to take this Byzantine tale: sorry, it has *absolutely nothing to do with anything*. But it gave us a chance to get a bit of local colour from Grenville and check up on Arthur.

I went back to the kitchen to see what I had done with my drink. I asked my wife at the sink, "Did you see my sherry?"

Without turning her head, she said, "The 'barn man' is back again, but looking far less troubled than before."

"Oh, that's good." I said, clutching at any straw.

"Do you mind if we settle up, sir? All's done. I've got everything loaded on my truck, and the contractor's boys will haul away the concrete if you ask them. How does £50 sound to you?" he asked, with a quizzical look.

It sounded rather a lot, and bearing in mind I was mortgaging my salary in all directions that afternoon, I decided to be a little more careful with my money.

"How about forty? How does that sound to you?" I asked sheepishly.

"That sounds just fine," he responded immediately, and to my great surprise, *enthusiastically*.

I *hate* bargaining, and here I was haggling like a master. With a similar interrogative glance, I said, to him, "I should have said thirty-five!"

Once more Sam Weller responded with gusto.

"No," I said, "I don't need change, I have it here."

"This ain't change sir," he said, "This is what I am paying you for those antique oak uprights we just loaded. Very much in demand they are, sir. Antique timber, sir – can't find it, sir. Here you are then, £35 as agreed." He counted notes into my hand.

It was no wonder he had been so happy to go along with my haggling, since he had managed to get me to haggle against myself. Of course, I was far too embarrassed to say anything, so I shook his hand, and with a deal of manoeuvring, he exited my grounds in his truck. I stood there, waving the £35 at him in farewell.

By now, the sound of tearing and ripping upstairs had been replaced by hammering – which is a positive sound in the joinery business. But wait, I was able to hear that because the compressor was off and the jackhammers had finished. Indeed, I could even hear the doorbell. Oh! The doorbell. Two gents in overalls stood there.

"We've broke it all up, and we will send a bloke with a truck to haul off the concrete. The firm will send you the bill. Lovely day."

Then they, too, were gone just as dusk was approaching. I turned to re-enter the house and walked straight into John coming out of the kitchen.

"All done, but you will need to paint and paper it. No problem there as Arthur is up there and that's exactly what he does, though he looked a bit dubious at the word *paint*. Glad to have been of help."

Before he could drive off, I said to him excitedly, "Wait. If you are leaving, that means that you have rebuilt the cupboard. And you could only have done that if the immersion heater had been *installed*." This Holmesian deduction was brilliant, I thought.

"You got it," a voice said behind me as a hand descended on my shoulder. It was Godfrey. "You are set to go, my lad. Have a celebratory soak."

With that he too started up his van and prepared to leave. After doing a swift calculation on my fingers, I realised that only Arthur remained.

I rushed up the stairs and to my amazement found Arthur packing up. He was able to do this because *everything* was papered.

"How on earth did you do that so fast?" I asked.

"Godfrey's good with a brush, and he got bored."

"Oh, so you're off. Well, send me the bill, and thanks."

With a wink, he said, "I didn't want to stay around, because I was starting to feel lonely. You know, you should take the day off tomorrow."

Then the last remaining vehicle left the yard. I returned to the kitchen to celebrate the triumph of having accomplished so much in the day. A sense of calm and order had returned, and the evening sky was a deep indigo shade behind the silhouette of our trees, slowly bending, hiding and revealing the brilliant early stars.

"Come and look at this," I urged my wife.

"Just a minute, I have to put the vacuum cleaner in the cupboard."

Then there was a crash as she displaced several things inside the cupboard.

"Hey!" I shouted. "You will injure yourself wandering around there in the dark. Put the light on."

"What light?" she asked, from the dark recess.

6

Up, up and... uh-oh

SOMEWHERE OVER NORFOLK, 1975

"VERY *FLAT*, NORFOLK," Noël Coward has one of his two embarrassed characters, on adjoining balconies, remark in *Private Lives*. There's no denying the truth of that, but Norfolk is not flat in the endless way Kansas or Iowa assume the horizontal. Here the results of centuries of settlement have produced hedgerows, sunken lanes, tree-lined country roads and a general 'rolling English road' environment that would have delighted Mr Toad. Excursions along these often ancient roadways are enlivened by the frequent appearance of timeless villages with impossible names: Little Hautbois,[9] Great Snoring, Puddledock, Wymondham, Potter Heigham, the glorious Wacton, Bacton and Aslacton, Dickleburgh, Happisburgh, Costessey, Pudding Norton, Seething, Stratton Strawless, and the wonderful finality of Trunch.

In the early autumn of 1975, while the evenings were still long and the colours deepened by the setting sun, my greatest pleasure was to cruise these lanes on my modest blue motorcycle and commune with Nature. After dark, the landscape assumed a more threatening appearance, which M R James used to good effect in his East Anglian tales of the supernatural. In fact one reading of *Casting the Runes* could have me in bed before sunset any night of the week.

But the September sun was still far from set when I went out for a rural ride at the end of one spectacularly beautiful day. As my colleague and sometime poor navigator used to say, "We're not really heading for anywhere, because then you cannot get lost." So, the drive was, as usual, aimless and meandering. It was not quite so easy to commune with Nature wearing a helmet, but it was a lot better than riding in a car, and a lot worse than walking.

On this occasion I saw a rather unusually large group of people in the grounds of a private school a few miles west of Norwich, and it became clear that they were not schoolboys, even though all this activity was taking place on the sports field. Because of the flatness so astutely observed by Mr Coward, I could not elevate myself high enough in the saddle to see the focus of their attention. So I slowly cruised in through the gates, parked the bike and sauntered over.

There on the ground, laid out like a giant's laundry, was an uninflated hot-air balloon; something I had never seen before.

---

9 Hautbois pronounced *Hobbi's*, Wymondham pronounced *Wyndham*, Happisburgh pronounced *Haysbr'a*, Costessey pronounced *Cossy*, Trunch pronounced Trunch.

The first question to ask was clearly: "Have they just come down, or are they going up?"

The answer came back: "Up, soon." Well now, here was a new, if somewhat anachronistic happening, and so I forgot my ride and settled down on the grass to see how it was done. I recognised at once Mr Birchmore, who was a student at my university at that time, and I remembered he had told me that he was a qualified hot-air balloon pilot. Frankly I didn't know such qualifications existed, but they do, just as there are qualified steam-engine drivers around.

Mr Birchmore, who – because of his name, I suppose – was studying Environmental Science, explained to me what was about to happen. The club that owned the balloon took people for trips for the modest fee of £5, to defray the expenses of maintaining and fuelling this monster. Two of his passengers were standing there: a rather large American, and what would have been called in Norfolk, a 'young lad', who looked in his early teens but was, it turned out, rather older than that.

Most activities of this sort ('barmy' my father would have called them), involve:

- the use of mystical words known only to the initiated (like yachting, which goes off entirely into its own language);
- an impression of tremendous animation and role-playing. I always think of it as 'unfocused animation', because it always ends up with the one person who has any idea what is going on saying, "Lift the bloody end or it will catch fire," or something like that;
- a sense of wonderment and awe on the part of the hoi polloi who gather to watch.

Frankly speaking, I don't think much of this has changed since the brothers Montgolfier sent a sheep, a duck and a cockerel up in a balloon on that first historic occasion in France. The choice of livestock was because the Montgolfiers were wise enough to know that the trio was quite possibly not going to return to earth in an ambulatory condition.[10]

First of all, some of the acolytes lifted the lower part of the balloon 'bag', as I foolishly called it. A large fan was used to blow air into the mouth of the balloon so that when it was partially inflated, hot air could be fed in. There was someone in there helping to spread the air around, and Birchmore told me that he was called 'Cremation Charlie'. While this poor sap was holding it up, someone lit a burner and a giant flame shot into the balloon. The acolytes had now assumed a much higher standing with the crowd because they were handling something that could kill you – even before you went up. My impression was that if you shot a giant flame into a balloon, it would burst into flames, and I was preparing my 'Hindenburg commentary' for when I got home. Nothing so dramatic occurred. All this hot air started to plump up the giant form lying on the grass, and it began to fill out like some primordial monster returning to life. Heavens, it was big.

Now it was really beginning to look like a balloon, and with all that hot air, it started to assume a vertical format, leaving me to wonder what was going to hold it down on *terra firma* while the passengers embarked. People hanging on ropes, as it turned out; but I had seen on old newsreel what happened to some of them in Lakehurst, New Jersey, when they didn't let go soon enough. However, that had been a matter of dirigibles, and people had been around balloons *much* longer. Right, here it was: a perfectly formed balloon, ready to go.

I forgot to mention one other characteristic of 'unfocused animation', and that is: at precisely the moment the man is supposed to jump off the Eiffel Tower, or plunge into a vat of burning oil, there is always an *inexplicable delay*. The most practised exponents of this art, wishing to distinguish themselves from bus drivers, which they really are, are airline

---

10 Actually, they survived in excellent condition, paving the way for manned flight.

pilots. They have mastered the art of the unexplained delay and raised it to a science. Don't you love the way airline schedules always say, 'Departure 9.06'. Not 9 or 10, or 9:30, but 9:*06*. You know for a fact that if they take off the same day you are in luck. Anyway, back to the balloon.

They were clearly wasting valuable gas, which they released with a huge whoosh every time the awe-level of the crowd threatened to wane. But even that was beginning to pale. By now I had reached that point of suspended animation that accompanies all these events, and was wondering how long I should go on waiting. Knowing the pilot, I was able to raise my street cred a few notches by ambling over to him (I was his Dean, after all) and saying:

"Birchmore, my favourite aviator, why are we standing around? What part of the ancient tradition are we missing?"

"We have been reserved to take three passengers, a full load, and as you can see, we have only two and I cannot imagine what has happened to the third. We explained very clearly that we cannot hang around because it burns gas to keep the envelope inflated."

I realised how close I had come to losing all credibility, as I had been about to refer to that huge structure as the 'gasbag'. The worthy Birchmore continued, "The problem is that we don't quite break even with two, and normally we have quite a waiting list, but now we have been compromised."

"Why don't you ask the crowd?" I enquired. "There has to be someone out there who is good for a fiver and would love an experience like this."

"Oh, I am sure – but there is a problem, because we cannot take people up unless they are wearing a helmet. It's the law, you know. The missing passenger was bringing his own, so I didn't bring a spare."

I could not help noticing the fact that, as he spoke these words, his eyes were fixed on the crash helmet I was still wearing to gain a couple of street cred points of my own.

"Oh no, no, not me!" I said to him immediately. "I am not sure about this eighteenth-century technology."

"Oh, come on," he urged, reminding me, "You are the faculty sponsor of the Hot Air Balloon Society, so it is your duty."

"I don't remember reading anything about actually having to get into the thing," I informed him, but by this time, two sturdy arms had gripped my shoulders, and I was dropped into the basket. The deed accomplished, Captain Birchmore welcomed me aboard. Still in shock, I didn't start reasoning with him, and so we cast off (yes, that was the expression he used). To my amazement and muted horror, I watched the people slowly slip away into the Norfolk evening far below us. I couldn't get that duck and cockerel out of my mind. But, after all, they survived.

Once I had recovered the ability to speak, I asked the pilot, "Where are we going, Captain?"

"Who knows?"

"Well, you are the captain, and even square riggers knew where they were going."

"It depends on the wind. At the moment we're heading slowly west – you see the people on the ground there behind us."

At this, something immediately popped into my mind, and I posed my next question.

"If we don't know where we are going, then how will we know when we have arrived? AND, how in hell do we get back? I mean, we could be anywhere by the time you put down. By the way, you *can* control the up and down on this thing, can't you? I ask because I see no controls or instruments. All I see is I am standing a bloody big basket, like a fruit."

"Remain calm," he said. "The rules are that someone will be following us on the ground – in fact, you see that red car? Well, that's our tracking team. We call them the 'Chase Car'. They have done this a hundred times."

"Good," I said, much reassured. "So let's hope the wind does not change and we go over the sea, because I know for a fact that that model of Honda doesn't do well in heavy seas."

But now, having cast my fate to the winds, literally, I began to look around. The panic subsiding, I came to appreciate that there really was something to this. During my anxiety attack we had risen a long way, and the landscape lay below us like a model. Birchmore had a map (but no means of communication with the ground), and used it to trace our route. He told me that on the trials of the ill-fated R101 dirigible in England, they had no blind radar, or any other sort of radar, and either used dead reckoning if they looked up,[11] or road maps if they looked down. On one trial they were caught in heavy mist and could not see in either direction. So they sent a lookout *down* on a rope (as opposed to up the mast). He had a telephone connection with the bridge, and when he was low enough he looked around for a landmark (can't do that on the sea). When he eventually came out of the cloud he found himself in wild moorland suspended over two motorists in an open tourer.

"Excuse me," he yelled and they looked around in all directions, to see – *nothing*. After a few tries he did get them to look up, to see this man hanging from a rope attached to a cloud. They did not wait around to give directions, and probably swore off drinking for life.

The amazing thing was that everything was so still. Apart from the odd moment when Birchmore whooshed the gas burners, we were travelling 'suspended in space'. Only the odd creaking of the basket provided noise to accompany motion. Also, there was no sense of lateral motion. I put my hand out to feel if the wind was rushing by.

"No use doing that," said Birchmore. "We are travelling *with* the wind."

"Quite so," I remarked nodding, having been caught out badly there. "It really is beautiful up here, amazing really."

---

11 He also told me that the R101 was still classified as a 'ship', not a plane. In fact no-one could work out what it was – it had a ship's wheel, naval ranks, rigging, etc., but it flew. They still had not worked it out when the R-101 crashed in France, after which the problem went away.

The bucolic charm of aerial rural Norfolk was momentarily interrupted by the end of the world. Suddenly there was a whoosh that Birchmore's burners could not have made if they had all blown up together. We started to spin around, and it smelled as though everyone's paraffin stove in the world had just exploded.

"What in hell was *that*?" I asked, desperately trying to maintain control.

"It's those American Air Force buggers. They are based near here and are always going out on exercise or patrol, or whatever it is that they do. Occasionally, when we are a little close to restricted air space, or when they are bored out of their tiny, gung-ho minds, they buzz us. But they are travelling so fast you don't hear them coming until they are almost under you, and then you get the backwash from the jets."

"The eighteenth century was just missed by the twentieth century, you mean?"

"That's about right."

I tried to focus on the calming influence of Constable's landscape slowly passing below. I tried to reason like a cockerel or a duck – they survived.

At times, Capt. B would allow the balloon to descend quite low to illustrate how wind patterns could change with altitude. I also noticed that when we came down, even if the jets were off, the cows and horses below went berserk, running madly in all directions.

"The thing you've got to watch out for here is power lines," the good captain remarked during one descent. We seemed at that point to have hit the Doldrums because we were stalled at low altitude and going nowhere. I asked Capt. B how we got out of this.

"Oh, I was just enjoying the experience of hovering over the ground."

"Actually," I observed, "You are hovering over a gentleman who is pruning his roses, I believe." I had never seen the world from this angle.

"That gives me a chance to confirm our location – I am not entirely sure where we drifted after we were buzzed."

I realised, with a sense of total déjà vu, that he was about to give us an action replay of the R101. "EXCUSE ME," he shouted, though it was a totally silent autumn evening. The man looked around him in every direction, except up, of course. Captain B repeated the call, whereupon the aged gardener looked around some more – checking out the interior of the privet hedge this time. Birchmore scribbled 'Look Up' on a piece of paper and deftly dropped it by the man's left leg. He didn't actually see it fall, but noticed it as he gave up his search and went back to pruning. He picked it up and stared at the words in puzzlement, until eventually, as instructed, looked up.

Now, if you have not seen four people in a fruit basket hovering over your head, then you have never been a serious drinker. Or, this could be how life ends – they come for you in a basket and throw you a note. The poor man was so disoriented by what he saw that he slowly fell over backwards onto the lawn. Just then a breeze blew up, which moved us sideways at a clip, toward new adventures. I suppose that when he opened his eyes to find we were gone, he assumed he had made it to Paradise, and it looked just like rural Norfolk.

Onward and upward now, sort of leap-frogging across the trees and hedgerows. No-one was paying attention to the time, until the American suddenly interjected.

"Can you put me down now? I have to get back to town."

I asked Birchmore how he was going to do that because at that moment we were in the middle of nowhere.

"Don't forget," he reminded me, "that we are being followed closely on the ground, and when it is clear that we are going to land, they will come to us. No place is far from a road. Also, I will play around with the winds, and see if I can put us down somewhere accessible."

He found his ideal spot fairly quickly and started an angled descent to where we could see the car had already anticipated our arrival.

"Now, pay attention," our Captain spoke up. "We are going to land, and contrary to everybody's ideas, we do not come *straight down*. We come down at an *angle*, even if it is not obvious to you. This means that when the basket touches down, the balloon still has some considerable momentum, and since *it* is not on the ground, it will continue in its existing direction until halted by the weight of the basket and the people. Now, understand this, this momentum can *tip the basket over*, which is why it has sturdy handgrips. So I want you to get down and grip them from *below*. Understand, *below*. And you do not – repeat, *do not* – let go until I tell you. Just let the whole thing settle down and use up its energy and everything will be fine."

So, we all crouched down, which meant we could not see the ground. Soon there was a thump as we hit the grass. We understood immediately why they used baskets, because they are so flexible that they absorb much of the impact. What happened next is the stuff of legend. The American let go of the handle at precisely the moment the balloon carried forward and tipped the basket. He was, in effect, fired out of the basket and landed heavily on the ground. I don't think I have to tell you what happens when you throw about fifteen stone out of a balloon. Right: it shoots back up into the sky, along with the chicken and the duck.

But that was just the beginning, for Bill the American had entangled himself in some piece of loose webbing, and now it was wrapped around his leg. He was naturally eager not to re-join us hanging upside down and twenty feet below, so he struggled with it while everyone rushed forward to hold the balloon down. He yanked on the strip to free it, and when he had finally freed himself, he said "OK". At that point everyone let go of the basket, and we shot up.

I have absolutely no idea how high we went, but very quickly the landscape had achieved model village proportions again.

"Great, that was quite a ride!" I commented, and would have said more if I had not become aware of the strange ashen colour of Capt. Birchmore's face. "I say, are you OK?" I enquired, though it was perfectly evident he was not.

"We are in a pickle," the Captain responded, which was, given the actual circumstances, something of a serious understatement. His eyes were fixed on the top of the balloon as seen from our vantage point. "I'm afraid that Bill, when he flew out of the basket, got caught up in the lines. It seems that in his thrashing around on the ground trying to free his leg, he was tugging on this lead."

I knew I did not want to ask the next question, but inquiring minds have to have answers.

"Is that bad?"

"Indeed it is, because he pulled on the line that opens the deflation port, which is a flap in the top of the balloon that we use to let the air rush out when we land. That way the balloon does not drag us around."

I followed his pointing finger up to the crown of the envelope, and there, sure enough, was a flap – not fully opened, but partially so, and with the force of gravity encouraging it to open completely.

"Rush out, you said?"

"Yes, and it is evacuating now at a fair rate, as you can tell if you put your hand over the edge of the basket."

Sure enough the air was rushing through my fingers from below. Rushing rather fast actually.

"Our only hope," (and I did wish he had not said that) "is to turn on the burners flat out and drive hot air into the envelope, at least to slow our descent, but I do not think I can compensate for the rate it is leaving."

"Compensate, compensate," I urged. Better that than telling us about it. Then came an almighty whoosh and flames were heading skyward and, I hoped, slowing us down.

"I say."

I turned around, having completely forgotten that there was a third person who was going to die with us, and I didn't even know who he was. Well, we had not been introduced, you see.

"Yes?" asked the captain of the fresh-faced lad.

"Just over there is a large expanse of water – a lake, or reservoir or something. Wouldn't it make sense to try and get over there and land on water? I mean, we could certainly stay alive until the Chase Car comes."

This made excellent sense, and I was impressed at the lad's totally calm demeanour. I looked at the captain for a response.

"Absolutely right. However, my main aim is to slow the descent – in fact, we are drifting in that direction, but I cannot place us over it in time, I fancy. So, listen closely because here's the score. We are going down much faster than is safe, and I don't know whether we are speeding up or slowing down, but I have to tell you this is a very dangerous situation. I want you down in the basket hanging on to the undersides of those handles. That is the safest place to be until all motion is arrested.[12] Throw all the things over the side that could fly about and hit you. Right, down, NOW!"

We immediately assumed the position, and hurled out everything. I was happy to have my helmet, though this was not what I had had in mind when I bought it. Birchmore, meanwhile was standing up, which couldn't be good.

"Get down man – you will be thrown out!" I yelled.

"No – if I am not standing with the gas control in my hand just before we hit, then we are *all* Cremation Charlies – you understand."

"Goodness, you are right," I said, rather embarrassed.

From the bridge, Capt. Birchmore alone could see our fate and would describe to us our last moments. At this tense moment, the lad – whose name, I am ashamed to say, I have since forgotten – made the observation: "I suppose I should be scared to death, and I never expected to die this way. But it all seems rather stupid, don't you think?"

---

12 Which is, if you think about it, another description of death!

"I think it's considerably worse than stupid," I replied, "My wife thinks I went out for a short bike ride before dinner. How is anyone going to explain that my body is now waiting for her, wrapped in a large plastic bag, on the side of a lake some place we have never heard of? She must already be worried sick. What do you see, Birchmore?"

Our worthy captain, preparing to go down with the basket, said, "OK, we are coming down at a steep angle and very fast. There is nothing more I can do. We are going to hit in a huge forest stretching as far as the eye can see. Big trees, so hang on because we may be tipped over. Right – here it comes!"

With that he shut off the burners and threw himself onto the basket's floor, hanging on for dear life. Well, actually, that was *exactly* what he was hanging on for. Now instead of the huge roar of the gas jets, we had total silence, and I remembered that the steam whistle (safety valve) had thundered into the night on the *Titanic* as it went down, until it stopped so that everyone could die peacefully. Death in the forest, I thought, was at least an appropriate way of Capt. Birchmore to end his aeronautical career.

The silence was extremely short-lived. There was a mighty crashing, cracking, ripping sound, and bits of branches flew everywhere, tossing us about like toys in a box. The basket was taking a tremendous thrashing, and then – nothing.

But five seconds later the base of the basket hit the ground with a thud. Birchmore leapt up and yanked on the line so that what was left of the air in the balloon rushed out. The envelope collapsed around us. But how could this be? Instead of staring up at a mauled forest, we were looking at an open sky.

"I don't suppose we made *that* huge a hole in the trees?" I asked the captain, who was looking totally astonished.

"Stand up, stand up!" he commanded, and we emerged from our burrow to look around, and we too were stunned. In thousands of acres of tall woodland, we had managed to land in the only clearing, where, it seemed, forestry equipment was stored. We had missed all the heavy machinery, and were lying upright, with the balloon undamaged. We were undamaged too, which was more important.

"You know, I did not see this clearing while we were coming down, so I cannot take any credit for putting us in here. But if you look at the trees you will see we clipped our way through the upper branches and that decelerated us before we touched ground. Actually, that was a softer landing than when Bill was shot out."

"What now?" I asked.

"Well, the Chase Car will have seen all of this, but of course they have no idea where we came down in the forest. Probably they are thinking the worst, and I am sure they have called the authorities by now. Still, we are lucky because there is a trail out of here, and so," (here he looked at me in my leather coat and helmet, feeling like Lindbergh in Paris), "you should hotfoot it down that trail and tell them where we are."

And so I set off. The sun was setting quickly now. In the forest, Constable was yielding to M R James very quickly, which provided a good incentive for haste. I felt for all the world like I was on my way to Grandmother's House.

Soon it became almost totally dark along the trail, but at least I had that to follow. Eventually, the trees started to open out a bit and there, ahead of me, I could see the moon reflected in the surface of a river. The track turned inside the forest to parallel the water, but I thought I would just check out the river, in case there was anyone around.

As I emerged from the trees, a cheer went up. A crowd was assembled along the riverbank, presumably alerted by the emergency vehicles. I felt like Dr Livingstone.

"Hello," I cried across the river. "We are all in good shape and we are in the maintenance clearing. If someone could explain to the Chase Car how to get there, we will wait for you."

With that I waved goodbye and wandered back into the by now totally black forest. Following the trail was not too difficult, and by the time I reached the balloon, Birchmore had everything neatly folded away. Then headlights started arriving and we were rescued. I was given a ride back to my motorcycle, where this whole fiasco had begun. I was still wearing my bike outfit, so I jumped on and rode home. All the way back, I worked through all sorts of fantastic opening lines: "I just survived a balloon crash", and so forth. As I pulled in, my wife heard the bike and came out to the door, no doubt distressed beyond words at my long, unexplained absence. I made a move to get off the bike, and fall into her tearful embrace.

"No, don't get off. We're out of milk."

7

Adventures in eating

ENGLAND AND WALES, 1950–1960

I WISH TO say right away, my recent visits to the UK have rendered inoperative all my previous biases and bombast.

What's mine is mine, and yours is mine too

Right away I am going to confess that I was not present at the following contretemps. So, although I can see these events unfolding, oh so clearly, within my mind, I am unable to claim authenticity – but they do sound exactly like my father and I will proceed on that basis. After all, he *was* the one who told the tale to me.

At this point in time I no longer have the slightest idea from which, and to which, train he was changing but that need had left him with time to kill at an intermediary station. Having secured for himself a copy of the *Daily Express*, he wandered over to the solid predictability of a British Rail buffet. This was in fact not a buffet at all, as I understand the word, but a café of a decidedly institutional nature that only the British have fully mastered. He bought a cup of British Rail coffee (unrelated to the drink of that name served elsewhere in the world) and a KitKat. We had not that long come out of World War II, and chocolate still had that 'forbidden fruit' allure that alcohol has on an American campus to this day.

After finding an empty table in the crowded buffet, he arranged his coffee and KitKat strategically around the central space to be occupied soon by that day's *Daily Express* crossword. The paper neatly folded, he placed it in its exact cosmic space, produced his pen, found the right angle for his bifocals, and set to work.

He was barely even aware of the fact that a man had quietly insinuated himself into the seat directly opposite him. The new arrival, rather unprepossessing and unremarkable, sat there staring at nothing in particular while he nursed his cup of tea. My father was having trouble getting started on this crossword and was further distracted, when, in his peripheral vision, aided by the striking colour of the KitKat wrapper, he noticed that his chocolate bar was *moving away from him*. The gentleman opposite, without a shred of furtiveness, opened the wrapper and neatly broke off one of the four bars of chocolate wafer with a reassuring snap. He inserted the piece into his mouth, bit it in half with another snap, washed it down with some tea, and noticing that my father was looking at him in blank astonishment, smiled a sort of Stan Laurel grin, and continued to demolish the remaining half of the chocolate finger.

75

Here we run into some British traditions that create a problem that probably would not arise elsewhere. First, it is considered unwise, and for that matter, ungentlemanly, to open a conversation with a total stranger unless the circumstances are dire ("Excuse me, I hate to intrude, but your wife has fallen under the train", for instance). Secondly, what the man had just done was so far off the scale of acceptability for basic British good manners that one had to at least entertain the possibility that he was an escaped, and quite possibly dangerous, lunatic. I mean, he was behaving in such a strangely calm and open way, while at the same time, stealing my father's food from his very mouth. What sort of man was this? Confronted with such bizarre and potentially alarming behaviour, Father did what any red-blooded British person would do: he pretended nothing had happened, and returned to the eternal search for a four-letter word (other than the one going through his mind), meaning 'reptile'.

Action, though, was clearly needed, so to establish the rules of territoriality beyond doubt, he reached over and pulled the KitKat toward him, loudly snapped off the second finger, and slowly chewed it to help with his thought processes. He consoled himself with the thought that at least there were two more left.

Imagine, then, his silent horror when Stan Laurel again reached over, smiled at him and pulled the KitKat all the way over to his side of the table, where he promptly snapped off the penultimate delicacy, and ate it, still surrounded by this aura of contented unconcern. Yes, this man had to be insane. Nevertheless, there were questions of possession, masculinity, territoriality and rights surrounding the last remaining finger of crispy chocolate.

Now, this would be a nightmare at the best of times, because the worst possible thing to happen during a meal in the UK, regardless of the presence or absence of dangerous lunatics, is to have *one item left over*. There are very precise rules governing this situation and they give rise to the following conversation, in this case concerning a dessert. But first, you have to recognise the undeniable and unrevealed truth that *each person around the table wants that last slice of jam roll.*

Host: "I say, Penelope, do have that last slice."
            [*encouragingly offering plate toward guest*]
Guest 1:   "Oh, Gladys, truly I couldn't. It's really delicious, and I've had two already. Thank you so much."
Host: "Well then, it's yours, Arthur."
Guest 2:   "What? Oh, no, no, no!" [*Much flapping of hands, followed by patting of ample stomach*] "Terrific roll. Really! Couldn't. Bloated you know. Go ahead, you have it."
Host: "Oh really, go on, it's only one piece. Just half, then?"
Guests 1 and 2:   "Phew, I'm stuffed. Really."
Host: "Well, I certainly cannot eat another slice, or even half a slice."

And so, it seems, it is destined to sit there for all eternity.

(Well, until the moment the guests go, when the host stuffs the whole thing into her mouth with a look of manic glee.)

There was, thus, in the buffet, a stand-off between my father and his opponent, easily as electrifying as Gary Cooper's showdown in *High Noon.* What would happen? The little fellow continued to sip his tea as though nothing was happening, though his look was not so much challenging or furtive as it was cautious, as though my father was the escaped madman. The nerve of it all. What was he playing at?

Anyway, this matter could not remain unresolved like the jam roll, for Heaven's sake. So, swiftly, my father reached across, grabbed the wrapper and demolished the last remaining wafer with vigour, making a definitive point as he did so. That done, he squared his bifocals defiantly on the fellow. Only now did his adversary show signs of some alarm. Quickly finishing his institutional tea in its solid proletarian white cup, he got up and left, with only one quizzical look over his shoulder.

"Enough," thought my father. "Someone has to stand up for their rights, or we will be trampled on. The War taught us about discipline and restraint," with a reassuring smile to himself for a job well done – a triumph for British firmness in the face of anarchy and an assault on all we hold precious. He returned to the crossword, determined to erase the foolish man from his memory. He was searching for a six-letter word meaning Andean goat when he noticed that it was almost time to board the train and complete the journey. Still pondering the missing word, he gathered up his paper, and was turning to reach down for his bag, when, its wrapper gleaming unmistakably bright red in his peripheral vision was... my father's KitKat, freshly released from under his newspaper.

Note: You may wonder how my father ever had the self-effacing grit to tell such a tale against himself, which he did in a very matter-of-fact way. This was achieved by deftly manipulating the English language to include the following phrase: *"and there it was, a brand-new KitKat* [here it comes] *he had left under the paper."* Of course, my father had laid out the newspaper long before the stranger arrived. No. Sorry Dad, that was *your* KitKat, but it gave us a great story, even leaving your integrity intact.

See if you can catch his eye...

This is a phrase uttered, maybe, ten million times every day in restaurants and cafés across the British Isles. This is a problem that defies logic, so I should try to explain the theoretical background.

If anyone from another country ran an eatery, particularly one where the clientele was seated and waited upon, they would try to make sure that, once the guests had finished eating, they would be hurried – very discreetly – on their way in order to make room for more paying customers. For some reason, this is not true in the UK, where once you are in, it is virtually impossible to get out because, try as you may, you cannot get the bill. We assume that mine host is, ultimately, after thy money, so what is going on here? There are several possible explanations, all related to well-defined characteristics of the British code of behaviour:

1. *Not Wishing to Intrude*
British people, in general, do not like to interrupt. So, for a waiter to come up to your table and bang the bill down would be a social faux pas of the worst order. You might have been on the verge of proposing to your intended, or your hand may have been wandering where it shouldn't, when you are suddenly startled, or compromised, by the arrival of the bill. Far better, thinks the waiter, if I just drift around on the periphery and leave them alone.

2. *A Class Thing*
Waiters are, of course, in a role of *servitude*, and this creates a multitude of problems for the very class-conscious British. You find none of the bonhomie that exists in the States where waitpersons (for Heaven's sake) first introduce themselves. Good Lord, thinks the average Brit, I don't wish to make friends of them – I just want my plaice and chips. Even worse, in America, these servers often drop to their knees to take your order. While in Britain the servile pose would be much appreciated, we are supposed to be getting a meal here, not becoming Catholics. So, rather than ruffle the feathers of representatives of a class clearly financially able to eat out, then it is better, the waiter thinks, that we stay out on the periphery and leave them alone.

3. *The Dignity of Labour*
You have to understand that capital-labour relations in Britain are both very ideological and class-based, and thus typically adversarial from the start. So, although servers may be willing to provide you with your food, because you are paying for it (and it boosts the tip if they are attentive), the bill represents

their lowly relationship to the capitalist who owns the eatery. The server thinks, "I have to grovel for a miserable tip, while the owner rakes in the profits from the outrageous price boosting on a glass of wine. I am oppressed." And so, collecting the money for the bill is an affirmation of this unfair division of spoils, the evils of capitalism, the crushing of the working class and many more ideological aspects that you never dreamed of when you were ordering the meat and two veg.[13]

Anyway, there are clearly several PhDs waiting to be garnered here, but we must move on from the realm of overarching theory to the much more mundane realm of practice: *What Actually Happens*.

Right, this is how it goes: The meal was fine (by British standards). As a long-term exile, of course, I am less than familiar with the quality of British cuisine these days. Suffice it to say that those two words would never have been put together when I was growing up. I once asked my brother, "What is the difference between a good meal and a poor meal in this country?"

"The price," he replied without hesitation. But we are wandering from our path.

There you are, wallet in hand, ready to pay, and now it is necessary to get the bill. You look around and find, to your astonishment, that all the waiters have been kidnapped by aliens, or are hiding under a table. This goes on for about ten minutes, and then one will appear like a target in a video game, vanishing almost as fast as you spotted him. The next one to come along is visible only to your partner, and if you are paying the bill, it is unseemly for the partner to draw attention to the fact that there is a money transaction involved. It has an aura of 'I am being bought' about it, and so it is totally unacceptable for you to show recognition of this patron-client relationship.

---

13 In America, where the needs of business are more explicit, things are a little different. In Bloomington, for instance, the waiters/waitresses in one eatery serve in T-shirts bearing the legend *Eat and Get Out*.

Since the waiter is now restricted to the line of vision of your partner, you have to make the first of your required statements: "See if you can catch his eye, would you, if he comes past again."

Now it is OK for the partner to make eye contact with the server. However, it is at this precise moment that the waiter leaves that area forever. Instead, he pops up once more in some distant corner of the restaurant where there are no diners and starts cleaning a long-abandoned table. From far away, he then turns and looks, almost, in your direction.

Now you have to resort to another terribly non-British pattern of behaviour, which is to draw attention to yourself. So you wave your hand in the air while saying, perhaps, "Excuse me", in a soft, submissive, well-modulated, and non-threatening tone of voice that the waiter is never going to hear.

The arm-waving, even if you set your sleeves on fire, will not be seen by the target of your attention. However, it will be seen by every other person in the restaurant, who all immediately stop eating, in order to fix you with an expression of undisguised disparagement. What you do not know is that servers in the UK, as a condition of their employment, are required to obtain Certificate of Eye-Avoidance from an approved institution. They wouldn't see you if you swallowed a hand grenade (though they would, naturally, wipe down the table afterwards). Ultimately, you go up to the bar or some other place that has a captive, non-perambulatory form of human, and offer the money. The reply to this demeaning gesture is: "You need to pay your server, sir."

The end result of all this is that by the time you *do* finally manage to obtain the bill, with its inbuilt 'service charge' (which is in no way supposed to obviate the need for a large tip), you have used so much nervous energy that you are ready for another meal.

Just such a thing happened in the 1950s when I was accompanying my brother and his wife on a trip to Cardiff – the diminutive capital of diminutive Wales. In this case, the server had more than fully absorbed the content of the courses at the Institute of Eye-Avoidance, because we were not able to make human contact even to obtain the menu and get started on the process.

We went through the whole gamut of gestures and waving, stopping short only of the practice at the Nairobi Hotel in Kenya at the beginning of the twentieth century, when a delay of this type in the dining room would be ended definitively by a guest discharging a revolver into the ceiling. Britain's strict gun laws prevent this course of action occurring in Cardiff, but we were at our wits' end. Another problem here is the fact that the British would rather die than complain. That is why you do not take anything back to a store for fear of being accused of damaging the goods and trying to pass off the responsibility, unforgivably, to the vendor. More astonishing to overseas visitors, if you *were* crass enough to complain about a meal, the server would argue with you:

Guest:	"The cream for the coffee is off."
Server:	"That cannot be possible, sir."
Guest:	"Well, look at the stuff floating around on the top – what do you think that is?"
Server:	"I am sure that is just the excellence of the cream in the milk, sir."
Guest:	"No. It tastes rancid and horrible."

At this point the server picks up the cup, takes a swig, his face becomes radiant, and expresses his total satisfaction with his judgment and the cream. Then, he defiantly replaces the cup in its saucer in front of you. Incidentally, you do not receive coffee 'refills' in the UK – and so, if you want to replace what the server drank, you will have to buy another cup. Since you know that the cream is off, this seems pointless.

Anyway, back to the plot. We had been accommodated in a corner of the restaurant as far as it was possible to be from the main circulation of the room. We had worked our way through all the various stages of eye-catching, excuse-me's and so forth, and nothing had helped. We were, effectively speaking, abandoned. We could no longer, even remotely, convince each other one more time that "he'll be along in a moment".

At that point, my brother rose and quietly left the room without a word to either of us. We assumed he had gone to the toilet. Meanwhile, our general situation remained unchanged: our isolation was complete. Suddenly, out of nowhere, not one, but three waiters appeared, materialising as though by magic from out of the walls. This was confusing, as now that this once-in-a-lifetime opportunity had presented itself, my brother was not around to place his order. What a paradox, for once these people left, we would never see them again. Interestingly, and very unnaturally, none of the waiters seemed that interested in taking our order, or leaving to hide, but instead were watching the door.

As though willed by their anxious gaze, my brother appeared, huffing and puffing and red of countenance. He placed his order, the phalanx of servers evaporated, and we sat back relieved.

"It's lucky you got back from the toilet when you did," observed my sister-in-law, "though it figures that they would arrive once you left the room."

"I wasn't in the toilet," my brother responded.

"Not in the toilet? Then where were you all that time?" she enquired.

"I was in the railway station," came his enigmatic comment, which mystified us.

"Why would you go to the railway station? We came by car," it fell to me to ask.

"I wasn't in there for the trains," he said, which, of course mystified us even more, since we knew of no other reason to cross the path of British Rail. "No, they have a phone box there – I remembered seeing it last time I was here. I noticed the number of this restaurant on the menu, and so I committed it to memory, ran to the station and called the manager to ask him to send someone to our table before we expired of hunger or old age."

"That was brilliant," observed my sister-in-law, and I had to agree wholeheartedly.

"Yes, it was rather bright," he chimed in. "And, even smarter is that I kept four pennies so that we are ready when it comes time to ask for the bill."

Putting on a good front

It was a perfect summer day. My good friend Roger (at that time at the Mathematical Institute in Oxford) and I set off to attend a wedding rehearsal in Worcestershire. I had more than a passing interest in this affair, because the wedding was mine. We made an early start and looked forward to a leisurely drive north-east from south Wales toward the English Midlands. Roger has never driven or owned a motor vehicle of any form or type, and so he is the eternal passenger (though, I must say, a good one – without any of those back-seat proclivities, or being given to sharp intakes of breath every time you pull up behind another car).

We had come, geographically, to the point where Wales reluctantly meets England at the market town of Ross-on-Wye: the River Wye being the border. Ross winds sharply down, via one sinuous, steep main street, from the ancient covered marketplace to the river below. We had also come, chronologically, to that part of the day then referred to as 'elevenses'. Under normal mundane conditions, this would be a short break for a cup of coffee and a smoke (remember, times were different then). However, when 'on the open road', as Mr Toad would have put it, elevenses moved a little further upmarket.

There, at the bottom of the hill, we saw it immediately. A quaint English tea-room (we were at least 100 yards into England now). I asked Roger what he thought, and he concurred that this was an excellent idea, so we parked and entered the establishment.

The place was everything you would have expected from the average time warp. It was set out with gingham tablecloths, faded local views dozed on the walls, and a deep sense of timelessness was startled by the old-fashioned bell above the door. Somewhere a clock ticked slowly, though without, it seemed, moving time forward. There was not a soul in the place, and we were intimidated by the silence, our British nightmare of having to make a collective decision about what to do, and the torpor of the environment. We stood there, looked at each other perplexed, and were just about to leave when the door to the kitchen, about halfway down the room and to the right, opened, and through it came the only possible person to complete this tableau – a sweet little old lady, who actually was wiping her hands in her apron as she entered the room. She suddenly became aware that we were there, for it would have been totally inappropriate for us to draw attention to ourselves. She raised her arms.

"Oh, my dears, I had no idea you were there, and here I am neglecting you. Come, sit down and tell me what I can get you to start this lovely day." (Her days started a little after ours – maybe it was an *English* thing?)

"Well, first and foremost," I began, "I know that I need a cup of coffee and maybe some toast."

"Oh, come now, that is not nearly enough, my goodness no. I think that toast needs an egg or two!" she said with a winning little-old-lady smile.

I relented, and Roger placed his order, which process included some banter, to which Roger is very susceptible if it is delivered by some Great Aunt-type figure who looks like she was delivered by Central Casting. Come to think of it, I believe that, via this time warp, he had been correctly placed in his true historical context.

"What a delightful place, and such a charming lady," he remarked. I nodded, though my attention had been caught by one curious anomaly. The door to the kitchen was on those swing hinges that, in Britain at least, we associate only with saloons in Westerns. It seemed so strangely out of place, and it emitted a grating squeak, similar to the kitchen door that featured unforgettably in Jacques Tati's immortal *Monsieur Hulot's Holiday*.

"It's awfully quiet in here," I observed, commenting more on the lack of business than the eatery's atmosphere of an undiscovered tomb. But I spoke too soon, for just then, emerging from the hidden kitchen, came the sounds of an argument in its early stages. It was not as though we could distinguish any actual words, just a general tenor of abrasive voices – both of them elderly; both of them women. Roger and I looked at each other with a smile and raised eyebrows: it was so out of place in this languid environment.

With that the squeaky saloon door announced the entry of our previous acquaintance (we never saw the other lady), bearing coffee and a beaming smile.

"This will wake you up, so you can make the most of this splendid day," she observed with the sort of gentle smile, head on one side, that made me wonder if she was going to ruffle Roger's hair – at which point he would have, as they say, fainted right away.

"Back with the food in a moment. You enjoy your coffee and let me know if you need anything." *Squeak*.

Before Roger or I could take the first sip of that steaming, much-needed brew, the unseen argument recommenced. It had changed into an altogether more aggressive pitch, and now the occasional word or phrase did escape audibly, such as, "That is entirely your fault: don't take that attitude with me."

"You should mind your own business."

We sat there, coffee poised twixt cup and lip, caught in that curious indecision that occurs when someone starts behaving in a decidedly odd way around you. Of course, *it was nothing to do with us*, but the continual rise in the pitch and fury of the argument was intimidating and uncomfortable in the stillness of the empty room; as well as being *totally un-British*. Plus, it was the sort of thing one simply does not do. (This was more than matched by the head waiter at a very exclusive restaurant in Cordoba, Spain. When I had ordered a fine entrée, I then said: "I want some green beans with that." "No, you don't. I could never be a party to that," was his stern reply.)

"I wonder what in the world is happening in there?" Roger asked. Before I could think of an answer, we were squeaked into alertness again. We fully expected to see the lady, bonnet askew, clothes mussed, and a fiery glint in her eye – maybe wielding a bloodied axe. No, she was as enchanting as ever; the big beaming smile, head cocked to one side...

"I popped some nice smoked bacon on there for you, too," she told me. "Now, you gents tuck in, and give me a call if there is anything you need, like more coffee. Anything."

I confess, the meal did look good, and wholly appropriate to such archetypically English surroundings.

"*Bon appetit*," I said to Roger, raising the fork charged with bacon in salute.

He never did get to reply, however, because from the kitchen came a storm of angry voices shouting and then the sound of dishes being thrown against the wall, swiftly followed by: "Get out of here!"

Bang.

"Do you think she is all right?" the ever-considerate Roger enquired, his head nodding discreetly in the general direction of the kitchen; a look of concern evident in his expression. "Sounded like the week's takings got demolished in there. Should we see if everyone is OK?"

Squeak.

"You gents OK? How's the bacon? Anything you need, remember, anything!"

Squeak.

"Eggs are good," Roger observed, one ear cocked for gunshots.

Foreign Parts

8

Why are you photographing that church? An innocent encounters Ohio

1964

MY FIRST FOUR visits to the United States – in the mid 1960s – were to Youngstown, Ohio; Sommerville, New Jersey; Little Rock, Arkansas, and Asbury Park, New Jersey. I have no explanation for this avoidance of everything worth seeing. The focus of this recollection is the Mahoning Valley in Ohio, which at that time still contained several flourishing steelworks and a healthy-looking economy. But first, I had to get there.

The student flight[14] from London landed in Montreal and I had to make my way from there by bus. In those far-off days, buses were still a respectable way to travel. An example of how far they have fallen since then was captured wonderfully by a Bulgarian lady who was waiting with me to collect her sister at a bus terminal in Indianapolis just after the fall of Communism. She seemed a little ill at ease, looking around worriedly, and then, with commendable Eastern-Bloc disdain, asked me, "Why is this place full of anti-social elements?"

I had been searching for the right term for years, and she hit on it first time, thanks to Mr Stalin. But in 1964, the bus was a perfectly acceptable way of seeing the United States, largely free of anti-social elements and, indeed, enemies of the people.

My journey from Montreal ended, as far as Canada was concerned, at the town of Trout River, New York. I know that because that is what it says in my passport. I had boarded the bus to Cleveland while still in Canada, and so our first stop was the immigration post. These were the days when visitors from the United Kingdom were required:

1. to have a visa;
2. to have declared, in writing, not to be, nor ever having been, a member of the Communist Party; and,
3. to testify that his or her purpose in coming here was not to assassinate anyone.

The bus duly paused but did not stop entirely, for the engine kept running, the driver's hand stayed on the gearshift, and everyone was clearly ready for an immediate departure. When the door hissed open, a very overweight gent in uniform slowly hauled himself up the steps. He exchanged a few pleasantries

---

14 BUNAC (The British Universities North America Club) would charter special flights so that students could benefit from greatly reduced fares.

with the two ladies in the front seat who, like everyone else in the bus, appeared to have been on a shopping trip, albeit an international one to Canada, where the US Dollar commanded a premium. Then in a very perfunctory way, the officer didn't so much ask, as sign out:

"Everyone here from the US and Canada?"

Above the head-nodding and general verbal assent came my voice, saying timidly, "No."

It was as though someone had let the air out of a balloon in a rush – instant deflation of the entire complement of passengers. All conversation ceased abruptly and the atmosphere dropped a good ten degrees. The officer looked down, defeated, at the floor and said, quite audibly, "Jesus Christ, there's always one."

Welcome to America. It didn't help that the address in my passport contained the words *Gwaelodygarth, Merthyr Tydfil*.

With that embarrassment behind me, I changed buses at Akron, or was it Toledo? Anyway, it was the place where we smashed into another Greyhound bus as we left the station, which meant we had to return for some sort of inspection. One thing I do remember is a little sign above the driver's head extolling something about the conviviality of travelling with this line, followed immediately by DO NOT SPEAK TO THE DRIVER. I recall that during this and every other bus journey, I never was able to engage a single person in conversation.

The arrangement was this: when I reached Cleveland, I would call my aunt[15] in Youngstown, who would then tell me the next step in travelling from Cleveland to Youngstown. She had already told me to be sure to have the exact amount in change for the telephone, and I was clutching it in my hand through most of the state of Ohio, just in case Cleveland suddenly appeared unexpectedly.

It eventually did appear, right where it was supposed to be, and we disembarked. I found the telephone, and (remember

---

15 She was not really my aunt, and in fact was not related to me in any way –
    Aunt was in this case a title accorded as a mark of respect.

what era this was) raised the operator, and told her the number. Miraculously, she told me to insert *exactly the amount I had in my hand*. I was thrilled that America was everything it had been cracked up to be. Then, thankfully, I heard my aunt's voice. She was really excited that I had made it, and began asking me this and that about the journey. Finally, she said, "Now listen, this is what I want you to do…"

I was never to hear the rest because, at exactly that moment, the operator cut in and asked, "Are you through?"

To me, having been raised with a different brand of English, this did not mean, "Have you finished yet?" – no, to me, she was asking "Are you *connected*?"

I was very pleased at her concern and happily told her, "Yes, we are."

With that my aunt turned into a dialling tone.

Let me recap. At this point:

- my aunt has no number for me;
- I have three $100 bills and no change;
- the link in my chain of command has been broken.

Knowing that all Americans are immensely rich, I assumed that changing the $100 bill would be a mere formality. In fact, the only way I could change it was to buy a ticket to Youngstown, which I did. I was told I could always get a refund.

Now that I had some change, I returned to the phone and called another operator, who, in turn called my aunt's house. There was no reply. I decided that the only safe option was to use the ticket I had bought since at least then I would be in the right place, and because I knew her address on Milton Avenue, I could take a cab to that very spot. So, I was soon on the next bus to bustling Youngstown. My aunt, however, unbeknown to me, was at the same time hurtling toward Cleveland in a huge black Buick with portholes.

Upon my safe arrival in Youngstown, I called my aunt's home once more. No reply. I decided to stick to my plan anyway.

The taxi duly delivered me to the door, where I offloaded my luggage, paid the fare, and prepared to wait for whatever would happen next. At least I was where I was supposed to be, the weather was fantastic and, best of all, I was in AMERICA. I settled on the veranda where, just as in American movie I had ever seen, there was a swing. I stretched out on it, and very soon was fast asleep.

A policeman prodding me and asking me what I was doing on the veranda rudely awakened me. I had been aroused from a very deep sleep, and so was not entirely compos mentis when he posed the questions, starting with "Do you live here?"

"No, I don't live here, but my aunt does," I explained.

"And where is she at this time?"

"I believe she must be on the way to Cleveland to meet someone."

"Who?" he enquired.

"Me," I told him, which immediately killed any vestige of confidence he may have had in me.

The situation was not helped by the fact that I was wearing an overcoat with a black fur collar – something my mother had insisted I bring, perhaps because she had seen Charlie Chaplin in *The Gold Rush*. The coat was much too big to put in the case, so I had draped over my shoulders. Since it could not have been less than 90 degrees in the shade, our conversation was not shaping up well at all.

At that moment, perhaps because the sight of a black-and-white patrol car was not that common in the extremely respectable Milton Avenue area, an elderly lady appeared, looking over the end of the veranda.

"Is there some problem here?" she enquired of the policeman.

Mercifully, the lady owned the house that backed onto my aunt's place, and it happened that they were poker partners. "Oh, he's OK," she reassured the policeman. "We were expecting him, but he was supposed to wait in Cleveland. I'll look after him till Dorothy returns. He's from England, you know."

She said it as though the policeman should know who Dorothy was without any further explanation, and hinted that anyone from England might well be strange. That satisfied the law officer, and he departed very politely. The neighbour, maybe to make me less visible and provocative, invited me around for some tea.

"What's with the coat?" she asked. About two hours later, my aunt arrived.

The plight of the obstinate pedestrian

By the time I had been in Youngstown for several weeks, my aunt had introduced me to American life with its walk-in refrigerators, huge basements, air conditioning and industrial-sized milk cartons. Interestingly, she had herself immigrated to the United States during the Depression. There, in Ohio, she had met and married a fellow by the name of Mike Sullivan, who really made good. At some point, he invented a dog lead attached to a long metal spike. When driven into the ground, this device allowed the dog to be secured, but at the same time it could run around within a fixed radius. This one idea that he turned into a home manufacturing business supported the family for the rest of his life, and beyond. He had passed away before my visit, but I remembered him from a trip he had made to Wales when I was about ten. He was a larger-than-life individual with gold spectacles and a broad fedora. But, in the depressed post-war days in Britain, he only needed to be American to be exotic. He liked to play at being the American that everyone in Britain expected, but he did it with such good humour that to this day I remember him very fondly.

That was a wonderful summer, even though the shock of Kennedy's assassination the previous November still reverberated, emphasised by the Johnson/Goldwater elections that were warming up. We passed the days with Art Linkletter, Ed Sullivan, and my first-ever sight of a colour television. I was also researching my undergraduate thesis in Youngstown, and so I was not short of things to do.

Although the details are hazy now, at some point I had purchased an 8 mm movie camera at the department store in the city centre. Because it had needed some kind of adjustment, I had to go back to collect it, which required a trip from the suburbs to the centre.

It was a stupendous midweek afternoon, and I looked forward to looking around, but first, I had to get there. Being a naïve European, I decided to use public transport. The question that concerned me was, how late could I stay and still get transport home? The movie *Quo Vadis* was playing and I wanted to see it. So I approached Aunt Dorothy for the answer:

"I have to go to the city to pick up my camera, and I thought I would stay awhile and see a film. But I will have to watch the time, so can you tell me what time the last bus is?"

She gave me a very curious look, and then, with the remarkably dry wit she could pull out of nowhere, she picked up the newspaper (the *Youngstown Vindicator*), appeared to study it closely, and then said, "The last bus left around 1957."

"You mean there are *no buses*?" I asked in disbelief, because, for a European, this was a totally incomprehensible situation.

"No. If you don't have a car, you are pretty well cooked, mister," she asserted. "Why don't I call your cousin Ronny, and maybe he can take you in his car?"

I told her that there was no reason to put him to all that trouble. I thought about how far it was, what a beautiful day it was, and made a decision.

"No. It's such a gorgeous day that I think I will walk."

"Walk!" she turned round in astonishment. "That's almost a federal offence.[16] I'm not sure you should do that, you might get lost and, especially round here, we have no sidewalks, and

---

16 Readers are reminded that this is pre-jogging America, long before the explosive growth of knee and joint replacement centres to treat all the 'keep fit' injuries to come.

so you will either be trespassing or jaywalking." (Jaywalking – walking on the road – is an offence in the US.)

This seemed ridiculous to me. I couldn't get lost as the way was simple, and if I did get lost I had the right coins to make a call to base (without the use of an operator). And so I set off.

I should have listened to Aunt Dorothy, who was a great observer of American life and its foibles.

My first problem was how to make my way out of the suburbs, but since they were much more attractive to walk through than the main street, I made a lazy saunter alongside the trim lawns and ranch-style houses that were the rage during that period.

I had not gone very far when a vast black-and-white police car (and they really were in those days) slowly cruised up to my side. To someone from Europe, this looked rather like the docking operation for the *Titanic*. The passenger-side window adjacent to me slid down with a mechanical whirr, and looking at me – at least, I assume he was looking at me – was a city cop wearing the mirrored lenses that I had never seen outside the cinema. Until then I had doubted whether they really existed at all; and here they were.

The ensuing conversation was very confusing for me, but possibly even more so for him. It ran more or less as follows:

"Are you in any sort of trouble?"

To me this seemed like a totally bizarre question. After all, what sort of trouble could anyone be in, strolling along in the sunshine without a care in the world? But this was exactly the inexplicable and aberrant behaviour that had caught their attention – I was walking.

"Trouble? No, I don't think so. Should I be?"

"Huh?"

"In trouble, I mean. Is there some sort of trouble of which I am not aware, maybe someone on the loose?" Now this really was turning into a movie.

"No, there ain't nobody running around crazy. I mean are you having trouble with the car?"

"Ah, I understand, and thank you. No, I don't have my car,"[17] I responded, very much impressed that an American cop should be so concerned.

"Is your car broken down? Did you leave it in a safe position?"

"No, it's fine and I remember locking the garage before I left." Though why on earth this would interest him, I could not imagine.

"Huh? So do you keep your car around here? What's the problem?"

"No, I keep it in Wales. I don't have a car here."

"You don't have a car?"

"No. Here, no. Not at all."

"OK, so what are you doing?"

"I am walking."

"Well, you need to be careful – you could get into trouble."

"Trouble? How?"

"Well, you could be stopped by the police, for one thing."

"I think we've already done that one. What else?"

"Where exactly are you walking *to*?"

"I am heading into the city," I replied, pointing in that direction.

"OK, get in. We're going that way. Just don't touch anything."

"Wow."

What a way to start a day! Pure Hollywood. I dared to suggest they might want to take me home too, but their shift was ending. Of course, how my aunt would react to *two* police cruisers calling at her front door in the same week was another matter. So after the movie, I started to walk back, sticking to the main street this time, and looking out for the landmark on the end of Milton Avenue, Mr Lasar's grocery store (he already knew my name and everything about me – in fact he knew it all before I arrived), where I would make a sharp left. En route, I

---

17 It was snug in its garage in Wales.

stopped at a bar, since that would be the normal thing to do in Wales, and there fell in with some wonderful rough and ready types, one of whom had a polar bear painted on velvet, which he allowed me to hold while he photographed me.

Saying goodbye to my new friends, I continued a little less steadily on my way, bearing left at Mr Lasar's. Aunt Dorothy was still quite concerned at the antisocial behaviour I displayed by openly walking all over the place, so the moment I got back she asked me: "How did your errand go? Did you find the city centre? How long did the walk take you?"

"Oh, I didn't walk into town. I was picked up by the police"

"WHAT!? Did they charge you?"

"No, it was totally free. Do they normally charge?"

"What on earth are you talking about? You were arrested?"

"No, nothing like that, they just gave me a lift, I think they had never met anyone who didn't actually have a car."

"Oh my Lord. But I suppose that's OK. Did the film end late? You are home rather later than you said."

"Oh, sorry about that, but I was carried away chatting."

"Chatting?" she enquired. "Who did you find to chat to?"

"Oh, these guys in a bar."

"A BAR! What in the world were you doing in a bar?"

"Well, I wanted to get a drink. That is what bars are for."

That's when she looked me square in the eye and said very sternly, "That certainly is not *all* that bars are for, and I recommend you stay clear. Respectable people don't go to bars."

That was when I came to realise that, in her opinion and by her standards, there was hardly a respectable person to be found in the length and breadth of Wales. I had never known that before. No wonder she had emigrated, Depression or no Depression – Herbert Hoover, here I come.

As a follow-up to this, one day while I was visiting my 'cousin' Ron, who lived in another part of the metropolis, I decided, despite all previous experience, to take a walk. At one point I came out at a major highway, and there on the other side was a shopping centre with a post office – exactly what

I needed. On the other hand, I could see no way to cross this highway that would not involve the services of a mortician. So, perplexed, I stood there for an eternity wondering where the pedestrian footbridge might be. I mean, there were people living in the houses behind me, and there were shops ahead of me. Surely the two had to connect somewhere.

Suddenly my attention was caught by a police car – flashing lights and all – pulling someone over. This was another piece of pure Hollywood for me, so I watched all the action until the culprit had been ticketed and allowed to leave. But before the officer could get back into his patrol car, I summoned all my energy and yelled, "EXCUSE ME!"

At that, he turned, saw me and shouted something I could not hear. When I cupped my hand to my ear to indicate my problem, he reached inside his car so that the next time he spoke, everyone the entire length of the Mahoning Valley could hear him. He had switched on the loudhailer on the roof.

"**ARE YOU IN TROUBLE?**" he shouted in bold upper case.

"No. I'm fine. How do you cross this road?"

"**WHAT?**"

"HOW DO I CROSS THIS ROAD?"

He paused for a moment at such a bizarre question, then raised the microphone and said to most of eastern Ohio: "**CAN'T HELP YOU BUDDY, I WAS BORN OVER HERE.**" He doubled over laughing at the might of his own wit. And then he drove off. I never did cross the road.

Later, my aunt expressed her opinion that I was having entirely too much contact with the law – three times now.

The case of the curious church

Cousin Ron (There are two Rons – father and son. So far I have mentioned the son; now we are shifting gears to the father), decided I should see more of the outskirts of Youngstown, in part because he had just bought a gull-wing-tailed Chevy

Impala in green, and was very proud of it. He even let me drive it. On the other hand he had been totally upstaged by Ron Jr., who was cruising around in a heart-stopper: a red and white 1963 Corvette convertible.

"Now then, young feller," said Ron Sr., putting on his movie voice, "We are headed for them thar hills. And that's known to be Indian country. Let's go. Mother, if we ain't back by Christmas, we died spreading the word."

This fellow was my absolute dream. He hammed up everything, and allowed you to do all the things that children are usually forbidden from doing on pain of death. Like shooting arrows at the washing. We rebuilt a pianola during that summer, and we would spend hours in the basement singing along – Ron Sr. and the young feller.

So he and I set off into the hills overlooking the industrial might of the Mahoning. We stopped to take a look; it was quite a view.

"Over there is Bethlehem Steel, Youngstown Sheet and Tube..." his arm waved expansively. "And, right there is where we live – see, close by those trees. I wish I had my binoculars to make sure that Billy is cutting the lawn like I told him. Ron goes to school over there."

"Does Ron have a girlfriend?" I asked, by way of conversation.

"Used to have. Used to. Really cute Greek girl."

"What? Did he break it off?"

"No. More like it was broken off for him when the family was blown up. The dad got into the car one morning and he disappeared along with the house."

I was not sure I had followed this conversation because this was Hollywood with a capital H. "What exactly do you mean, 'blown up'? Like a gas leak?"

"Well, young feller, you could call it that, indeed you could. Round here, on the other hand, we would call it M–A–F–I–A. This is Youngstown. Did no-one ever tell you about the Mob? It is one of our principal industries."

This was taking me into "WOW!" country, and no mistake.

"Great Scott. The Mob. Really? Where did the girl live? I mean, was it in Youngstown?" I asked in breathless excitement.

"Right at the end of our street; which, of course, is a little bit shorter than it used to be, if you get my meaning." He had huge brown eyes, and he used to do the Harpo thing with them.

So, after I had gathered my wits, I told Ron I was going to walk a little over to the right where there was a more commanding view, and I wanted some pictures for my dissertation.

"Good thinking, Tonto," he said, "I will cover your rear by sleeping right here."

I wandered over. It was an almost perfect evening up there on the hill: great visibility, very still, and almost silent. My father had lent me his camera, which I think at one time must have belonged to Mr Fox Talbot himself, because it had more dials than Mission Control. I was concentrating closely on focal length, depth of field and all those things when I felt the sky cloud over. "Drat," I thought, and looked up. The cloud turned out to be rather small, and shaped exactly like a severe woman in a severer black outfit. Blackest of all though was the expression on her face. She scared the wits out of me when I looked up.

"DDAAAGGGHHHH!" is more or less what I think I said, but she was totally unmoved, both physically and spiritually.

"Why are you photographing that church?" she snapped. She could have posed the question in Swahili for all the sense it made to me.

"Church? What church? I was photographing the steelworks in the Valley," I protested, and anyway, what *church* was she talking about?

"No. I saw you quite clearly and you were photographing the church." I strained my eyes to see if I could locate the church down in the valley.

"No, not there. *There!*" and she pointed a finger.

Lo, and behold, there indeed *was* a church tucked away in the trees not too far from where we were standing. "Oh no, I assure you," I protested, "I didn't even notice it was there, and I certainly was not photographing it."

"Yes, you were. I saw you."

"No, Madam, I assure you I was not, and if I appeared to be, it was without any intent. Anyway, even if I was, what is the problem with taking a photo of the church?"

"*That* church is under a Court Injunction," she stated firmly, as if that was supposed to mean something to me. "It's a very contested place. People photographing it are up to no good."

Then she looked me up and down. I was wearing my college blazer, which was not a common sight in Ohio. She immediately suspected that I was not only up to no good, but probably a *foreigner* to boot. This put the event into something of, quite possibly, international dimensions. Remember the Cold War?

"And anyways," she concluded, "You ain't from round here, so where's you from?"

"I am from the United Kingdom," I proclaimed proudly.

"Aha!" she exclaimed, totally vindicated, "Just as I thought. What is that? Some sort of religious institution?"

There was no easy answer for that, but fortunately Ron had awakened and was now standing behind her.

"Son, I've been watching you photographing that church for some time, and as an officer of the Federal Government, I must ask you to come with me peacefully. Thank you, Ma'am. You did your country a great service."

Before she could utter a sound, he dragged me off, muttering "Danged furners coming here and creating trouble for everyone." Then we jumped in the car and took off in hysterics.

9

Two cups of coffee,
a brown paper bag and
a magic carpet or two

MECCA, 1981

THE FOLLOWING TWO incidents are true, but in the way of explanation I offer nothing. I did not understand what was happening then, and time has not brought enlightenment, but this is an account of what took place. The circumstances are not as directly significant to me as, for instance, the previous story, because I was not present when some of the key incidents occurred. Inexplicable, nevertheless, they remain.

At the time, I was working in Jeddah, Saudi Arabia for a well-known British firm of architects and planners.[18] Looking after the daily administrative routine of keeping our office up and running was a very able man named Alayan Husseini.His passport was Jordanian, his nationality Palestinian, and his lineage was that of the notorious Grand Mufti of Jerusalem who had aged many a British official during the time of the Mandate in Palestine. That was by way of introduction, for Alayan was one of the easiest people to work with, endlessly charming and with a light sense of humour.

The latter was not much in evidence one Wednesday morning when the normally rather torpid ethos of the office was disrupted by excitement and many comings and goings by members of the Saudi Police. These were generally very diminutive in stature, wore unbecoming berets and patrolled in pairs, hand in hand. Once the office closed for the afternoon *siesta* as the outside temperature rocketed, I made my way to Alayan's office to satisfy my overwhelming Celtic curiosity.

"What's going on?" I asked a rather forlorn AH, as he sat in the perpetual gloom of his interior room.

"The worst, just the worst," he moaned, looking at the surface of his desk.

"Yes, but what sort of worst? Are you in trouble?"

"I may well be, because some time between yesterday evening and this morning, a big bundle of cash vanished from the safe. I don't know who is accountable for this. I have no idea how it could have happened."

I was rather astonished by this because burglary, and theft in general, was almost unheard of in Saudi Arabia – possibly because of the draconian penalties if you were caught. Your left arm would be considerably shorter if the law caught up

---

18 My responsibility for the company was 'the Region', by which is meant all those places without running water and other amenities.

with you. Indeed, the tales of honesty were legion, and went back to the conquest of the Hejaz[19] in the 1920s. On that occasion, Abdulaziz ibn Saud, the new ruler and conqueror of the Hejaz, decided to investigate the rather tawdry reputation of the Hejazis, who had been terrorising and robbing *hajjis* (pilgrims going to Mecca) for centuries. To this end he left a large box of gold in a very conspicuous street in Medina, where the Prophet is buried. The citizens of Medina, keen to prove their impeccable honesty, turned up with the chest at the residence where the new king was lodging. The conversation went something like this.

"Great King, we bring you as a token of the honesty of the good people of Medina, this chest that was found in the street this morning. Clearly someone has lost it, and it is a fine chest, so we bring it here for safe keeping under your protection."

"I am impressed," the imposingly tall king replied. "But it seems like a rather ordinary, though well-made, chest. Perhaps it would be best to return it to the place you found it, for who knows, the owner may be searching high and low for it as we puzzle over it. I appreciate your gesture, but I fancy I cannot trouble myself in seeking the owner of so modest a possession."

Then, to play their trump card and show *just how* honest the good people of Medina were, the leader of the delegation looked at the king, and said, "But Your Majesty, we cannot take it back because it is filled with English gold coins. There is a veritable fortune in here!"

To which the young king replied, "Really! How fortunate then that you found it. However, I must tell you that when I deposited this chest in the street this morning, I left it *locked*."

Anyway, fifty years under the strict eye of the Wahhabis had swept such weakness from the land, and so the theft of money

---

19 The Western part of Arabia containing the Holy Cities of Mecca and Medina. Until the mid 1920s it had been ruled by the Hashemites, until Abdulaziz ibn Saud and his Wahhabis swept out of the desert and put the Hashemites on notice. It became part of a joint Kingdom of Hejaz and Nejd, which then became part of the Kingdom of Saudi Arabia in 1932.

following a break-in was almost unheard of. My first thought was that this was an inside job, maybe by someone tainted by Western weakness?

"What now?" I enquired of Alayan.

"Of course, we reported this to the police – we could hardly do otherwise. And they came in droves, maybe out of a sense of the novelty of all this. But, you see there is a problem being in a land that is basically so honest. The police have no experience of solving crimes because they don't run into many."

"Hmmm." I pondered. "I never thought of that. It's a curious situation."

"Right," said Alayan. "So what happened is that the officer came here and wanted to know who had been around since the last time the money had been seen, which would be last night when I locked up."

"Well, that seems like standard procedure to me, Alayan."

"No, because then he said if we wanted to press charges, it would be his duty to take *everyone* on that list, and stick them in jail until the crime was solved."

"Hold on. That could produce a few problems, especially if, as you say, they have no experience in solving crimes. You could be there for ever!"

"No. *We* could be there for ever."

"Not good, Alayan, not good at all. So what are we going to do? Is the money a write-off, then? Seems like a Catch-22 situation to me."

"It is, and at the bottom of it all is the fact that I am responsible. If we get the police on the job, I go to jail. If we can't find the money, suspicion will rest on me, especially if nobody is looking for it."

"By gum, you're right – it does not look good for you. Do you have any ideas? I have never seen you at a loss for ideas."

At this point Alayan delivered me a curious, testing sort of look, before leaning forward and saying, "Soothsayer."

"I'm sorry. I thought they went out with Julius Caesar, omens and portents, and all that. Where do soothsayers come in?"

"Oh no," Alayan responded vigorously, "not here. I believe this may be the only way out, and I intend to take a taxi to Mecca this afternoon, and see what they have to say."

"That is a capital idea, especially since there seems to be nothing else we can try that doesn't put you in the pokey for the rest of your life. That can't be good."

"No, it isn't. Do you know your relatives have to bring food for you, otherwise you could starve in there?"

"Really? Do you want to tell me what you like to eat, because I know for a fact you have no family here."

"No, I am definitely going to do the Soothsayer thing. You know my father had a problem like this, and he went to a Soothsayer, and the man told him the answer to his problem would come to him in a dream that very night. And it did; it was revealed to him by a donkey on the roof of the apartment opposite."

"I thought that sort of thing only happened in movies," I said, thinking of Francis the Talking Mule.

"OK. Well, I had better go if I'm going – it's over fifty miles. I should be back early evening. Will you still be here?"

"This, Alayan, I would not miss for anything."

Off he went into the blazing noonday sun, heading east up the road to the Holy of Holies. And, true to his word, he came back into the office around five, looking much relieved.

"So, what did he say?" I asked from the edge of my seat.

"He told me to drink a cup of Turkish coffee, but only to drink half of it. That I did, and then he said 'What do you see?' I had no idea what he was talking about, until that is, he pointed at the cup. You know, real Turkish coffee has a slightly oily film on the surface, and he told me to concentrate and stare at that. I did, and I saw a picture emerge of this very office."

"You did! Fantastic. Did you see who did it?" I asked, totally caught up in this extraordinary event.

"No, I saw me, sitting here, and suddenly the door flew open and this man, someone I never saw before, and so did not recognise, rushes in like his pants were on fire."

"Given the circumstance," I observed, "Maybe they were."

"No, I could not *hear* anything, but he looked like the devil was after him."

I said nothing to that remark.

Alayan continued in an excited voice, "I asked the Soothsayer to tell me the meaning of what I saw, as I had no recollection of this event having happened, otherwise I would have recognised the man. The old fortune teller informed me of something very strange. He said: 'No, what you see is what *will be*, tomorrow, mid-morning'."

"Really, you were seeing the future? Wow. I think you know where I am going to be tomorrow morning, whatever else is on the agenda."

Not surprisingly, we kept the whole tale to ourselves, but predictions rarely come in full colour and with a timetable. We could hardly wait.

And so to bed, but I could not get out of my mind the very earnest way that the extremely pragmatic Alayan had recounted this fantastic tale – even though it lacked any talking animals. Well, the coffee cup had no soundtrack, so we couldn't *entirely* rule that out.

I had a definite sense of the Julius Caesars going to the office the next day. My eyes were peeled for portents, birds with snakes and the like. This is not a good idea given the combination of fatalism and craziness that guides the hands of Saudi drivers – and their feet too, come to think of it.

"Anything happened yet?" I asked Alayan, as I poked my head around his door.

"It's eight thirty," he remarked. "Remember, it was supposed to be mid-morning."

"I know, I just thought there may have been a trial run or something." There for an eternity we delved into the topic of precisely what 'mid-morning' conceptually equated to more prosaically in terms of hours and minutes. The answer came with a sudden crash that threw us all sideways, and provided us with the answer – mid-morning is 11.16 Mecca time.

Standing before us was a total stranger, a Yemeni, who began to rattle on nineteen to the dozen. Even when the Fates tell you something is going to happen, there is always an element of Cassandra about it, and I suppose, rationally, we did not really expect *anything* to happen. But this put Alayan clearly into a state of shock.

"Who are you?" he asked in Arabic. He went on to question the man rapidly and with rising surprise, and then said, "Come on", and off we went. To the beach. *The beach?*

There the Yemeni proceeded to dig in the sand, until he came up with a bankroll – a sizeable bankroll. He handed it over and immediately ran off.

"Hey, we never asked him why he came back – after all, he had the money."

"He said the devil was after him," Alayan observed, tossing the bankroll up and down in the air, and watching the retreating figure.

"Plus he gets to keep his left hand, which is always useful. I can't believe that all that stuff you saw in the coffee came true."

"It is a question of what you believe," he said, in a rather confident and superior manner.

The police found nothing unbelievable in the story, and left, since the money was back where it belonged.

The strange case of Bert's Carpets

What tale coming out of Arabia could lack a carpet? The carpet, or carpets in this case, were the normal 'stay still on the floor' type rather than those that predated the airlines. They were the pride and joy of a large, lugubrious South African planner on the team by the name of Bert Zank.

Bert had a passion for rugs and carpets, and Jeddah in 1971 was a good time and place to pursue that interest. Many of the *hajjis* making their once-in-a-lifetime pilgrimage were people of very modest means. They had developed a tradition of bringing with them things to sell to help finance their sojourn in the Holy Land. By this means and others, Bert had a rather splendid small collection, and he had assiduously read up about them.

Bert surprised us one morning by saying that he had been burgled, and several of his choice rugs had gone. He was about to head off to the police. I mentioned to him that his family would be serving time if he did that, and maybe he should have a word first with Soothsayer-General Alayan. I explained what had happened about the money, and Bert looked as though he thought I had gone soft in the head.

"Try the coffee cups," I suggested. "Oh no – you can't, because you are an Infidel and may not pass through the gates of Mecca. But Alayan can."

"I don't suppose I have anything to lose," he said and headed off for Alayan's retreat. I joined them.

Alayan said that there was a good chance that this would work, though it was a sort of 'third party' arrangement. He had some concern because Bert could not be there in person to divine the dregs, and none of us knew whether the coffee worked on a proxy basis. Anyway, Alayan assured us he would give it a try. Bert gave him the taxi fare and once again he departed eastward.

As before, Alayan was back in the early evening, this time carrying a brown-paper bag. It contained a white powder, which he told Bert he was told to sprinkle in the locations at home where the missing rugs had lain. He did this, rather self-consciously, and I cannot remember at this point in time whether he had to perform any incantations or rituals.

The very next day, he got a call to say that the police had spotted one of the rugs in Ta'if, the mountain station above the coast of the Hejaz. Bert drove up there, and, in company with the officers of the law, he found all his rugs, stacked in a pile of other rugs, in a shop. The police asked him if he wanted to press charges, and he said he did not, because we would be back into severed limbs again. He was happy to have the rugs back. Nobody could recall any time when the police had located stolen property before, never mind *overnight*.

10

The case of the
homicidal optometrist

CALIFORNIA, 1983

THE FLIGHT FROM the Fiji Islands to Paris is, I believe, about as far as one may fly without starting to come back. It looked like a life sentence until a friend suggested breaking the journey by stopping off somewhere new for a few days.

"Didn't you tell me that you had never been to California? Why don't you go there and stay with my sister? She would love to see you and take you around. I'll be happy to ask her if you like."

That sounded like a good idea, especially since I had not made my travel plans at that point.

So it was arranged that I would stop over in Northern California with the lady lawyer I shall call Julia. I had, in fact, met her before, though not in California, and so I didn't feel as bad as I would have about dropping in on a total stranger. She, in turn, informed me that she would take some time off and we could visit the vineyards of Sonoma County, and more. But first, I needed a booking.

The travel agent in Suva, Fiji, was adept at squeezing his clients onto already crowded flights, but he never explained how he did this. He told me that the time I requested was a "real problem", but he was working on it. Apparently his work paid off, because he called me to say that I was booked on Air New Zealand on precisely the date I wanted, aboard its flight from Auckland to San Francisco, via Hawaii, stopping at Nadi[20] Airport, Fiji.

On the appointed day I checked in, and the counter clerk offered her sympathies. I was too surprised to say "For what?" and so just thanked her. Once we were aboard Air New Zealand and headed for the International Date Line, the passengers settled in, and the purser came through on the public-address. I knew we were in for a different kind of flight when he said in a very gay and endearing tone, "Welcome aboard to all those who joined us at Fiji. I would like to introduce you to your cabin staff, who are here to look after your every need." He then proceeded to name the staff, and continued, "My name is Desmond. I was born on a remote farm in beautiful South Island, where I grew up with my sisters Alice and Leonora. At five I entered Infant School, and I remember it as though it were only… No, only kidding, folks."

It was not long afterwards that this same funster grabbed my elbow and said, "Mr Baker, I can't tell you how sad we were

20 Pronounced *Nandi*.

to hear about your father's terrible accident. I just wanted to let you know that all our thoughts are with you."

I could not quite place what accident he had in mind, first because I had heard nothing about it, and second because my father had passed away in 1978. Then it came to me that my travel agent must have spun some graphic tale of a fatal encounter with farm machinery or the like to get me into the seat that I occupied at that moment in time and space.

"That really is very *sweet* of you all to care," I responded looking suitably bereaved. Actually, this was a manoeuvre my late father would have very much appreciated. In the name of his doubly-departed spirit they brought me far more than my fair share of spirits. Because of this, I have no recollection of Hawaii at all.

Dawn broke over the spectacular California coast and there was San Francisco spread out below me. Though Julia did not live in San Francisco, but in nearby Oakland, the city was the nearest port of entry. I had just managed to compress my remaining double-vision into near-clarity in order to see the Golden Gate when we were down. Things in those pre-paranoia days were more relaxed on the airlines, and once you were out of customs there everybody was. Gradually passengers and friends paired up, hugged, and exited. Not me. This was shaping up like another familiar airport ritual: standing by the baggage carousel. It goes like this:

1. You take up your position at the one solitary remaining spot furthest from the rubber flap through which the bags will first appear. All the other places have been taken, even though you were first off the plane. Even the lady in the wheelchair has a choice position near the front.

2. You stand for an eternity while the same three bags go round endlessly, probably provided by the carousel manufacturer to inspire some sense of hope, or to have a good laugh at our expense. Those bags will still be there when you leave.

3. The bags from your flight start to appear, all piled at first into a crazy heap. Immediately, septuagenarians struggle to twist and lift their 90 kg suitcases. By the way, 'twist and lift' is the classic movement for displacement of discs in the spinal column, so the designers of these carousels annually receive a huge payoff from the chiropractic profession.

4. Your bag never appears. Though in fairness, on this occasion that was not the case, and it eventually emerged. It was, you will be reassured to know, lost on the next leg.

And so, back to the Arrivals Hall. By now, almost everyone has gone. I was looking for a smartly turned-out lady lawyer, who in my experience was normally attired in a grey suit. Nothing like that was anywhere in sight. In fact, the only remaining person not clearly affiliated with the airport's operations was in the corner, missing only a 1,000cc motorcycle to complete the look. The figure was clad in black leather, sported wrap-around sunglasses, and was topped off by a spiky hairdo. On the other hand, this apparition was looking at me and – was I wrong, or was I being furtively signalled to approach? I went closer, and was greeted with a hissed "Randall?"

"My God, is that you, Julia?" I asked.

"Ssshhhhh," she responded through clenched teeth, and motioned with her punk hairstyle that I should follow – at a distance.

Once we were outside, she led me to a venerable Volvo leaking oil – no motorcycle in sight. I tossed the bags in the boot, got in the car and off we drove off to some lesser-known part of San Francisco. She looked tense, and on the alert. This was not the woman I remembered.

We stopped eventually near a small, very unremarkable café, which she motioned me to enter. After glancing around, she then led me furtively to a booth at the far end of the establishment.

"What in the world has happened?" I asked incredulously once we were inconspicuously seated. "When did you go punk?

And why? I would never have found you if you hadn't identified yourself."

She did that stealthy over-the-shoulder thing that I had only seen previously in movies. Then she leaned across the table, fixed me with a determined look and –

"What can I get you guys?"

Julia jumped. "Oh, a couple of coffees – regular, strong."

The waitress left, and Julia resumed her conspiratorial lean across the table.

"We have a problem," she confided.

"How can I have a problem?" I asked. "I only just got here."

"We can't go back to the house. It is too dangerous!"

"Back?" I said, really confused, "I've never been there."

"No. I mean we can't go there, period. Look, here's the situation, then you can decide what you would like to do."

She then launched into the most bizarre tale I had heard until then, but as I later came to appreciate, it was perfectly attuned to California. It had a very high sense of earnest barminess coupled with mayhem. This, more or less, is what she told me, with a short break as the coffee arrived.

"I was defending this optometrist," she started, and that was a pretty good West Coast start. "His name was Ben, and anyway, to cut a long story short, we got sort of 'involved'. Of course that was a bad move and stupid, but, you know, these things happen." Actually, I didn't, but she continued nonetheless.

"He turned out to be *very* possessive and things began to get out of hand."

"Excuse me," I interjected, since I thought the next piece of information might be critical to the scenario. "What *exactly* was Ben accused of?"

"He was a repeat child-molester," she explained.

"Great. Continue."

"Anyway, he began pressuring me to let him move into my place. I didn't want any part of that, plus someone involved in the case would surely notice – it isn't entirely ethical. So, I told him it was impossible, but he would not take no for an answer.

Well, after I turned down his offer, he came up with a scheme to convince me that I needed him there with me. He arranged for one of his friends to come round and break in while I was there to make me realise that I needed a man in the house. What exactly he was supposed to do once he had broken in, God only knows."

"If I can make an observation, Ben doesn't sound like your typical optometrist," I ventured, "They are usually rather diminutive, in my experience."

"Well, he qualified in optometry while he was in jail, learning lots of other things as he went along," she explained. "But let me finish."

"Sorry."

"So, the other night this bozo, at Ben's urging, tries to jemmy the kitchen door. I heard the glass break and I crept in there to see this arm reaching in through a shattered window in the door for the lock. Once he released that lock I was chopped liver. I kept my head though, opened the drawer and took out a knife and nailed his arm to the door."

"*What?*"

"He was shouting and screaming like a stuck pig and there was blood everywhere. This scared me even more, and he was shouting terrible things, like what he was going to do to me once he got his arm back."

"God! That must have been terrifying? Weren't you scared stiff for your life?"

"Yes, that's what made me panic completely."

"But, you are here today, so you must have come through the ordeal OK. What happened?"

"Well, I shot him through the kitchen door with the shotgun I keep in the bed. After the second shell he shut up, like, totally."

Speechless. Brain in overload mode. No retort. I had never had a holiday start with a tour guide who had just shot someone with a 12-gauge through the kitchen door.

"Anyway, Ben was madder than hell because this guy nailed to my kitchen door and partly separated at the middle was some sort of school friend or jail mate of his. He died still nailed to the door. Anyway, Ben went totally, you know, gaga."

There was one question nagging at the back of my mind. So I interjected and said: "*When* did this happen?"

"Two days ago. Anyway, he called and told me he was going to kill me because of what I had done to his creepy friend. He was totally over the top – like raving. I took off immediately and went into hiding."

"Ah," I said, "and that is why you are decked out in this bizarre, but actually very fetching leather get-up," I said, now understanding all.

"That's not the whole of it. Yesterday he went round to a girl friend of mine – we always hang out together – and tried to force her to tell him where I was. She didn't."

"Brave girl," I said.

"So he killed her with an axe."

"I see, so he is really serious about this thing." I was now in shock, hence the banalities, which must be my way of coping.

"And how. I just know he is checking out the house, so that is why we cannot go there. But I don't want to mess up your holiday."

"How thoughtful of you," I ventured. "Where does that leave us – holiday-wise?"

"Well, he must not see us together because not only is he out to kill me, but he will be insanely jealous if he sees you. So we have to get out of here. We can take off for Sonoma right away if you like."

"Sounds good to me." Actually, somewhere more like Bolivia was starting to look even better. But then I had no idea where Sonoma was anyway.

I thought I had heard the whole story, but I was wrong, for she leaned across the table in, if possible, an even more conspiratorial posture, and asked me, "Do you have a briefcase or bag that you can carry with you?"

I put my black briefcase onto the table.

"Open it," she said, so I did.

With that she dipped into her handbag and pulled out a very substantial revolver. I was supposed to slip it slyly into the Samsonite bag like they do in the movies. Instead I found that my lower jaw was in the way. Europeans are not as familiar with portable artillery as our cousins in America.

"NOW!" she said in a shouted whisper. So I scrabbled it into the case, and snapped it shut.

"I feel better now that you have that," she commented.

I didn't.

"But," I asked, "shouldn't *you* have this because you can recognise him, and he is primarily after you, remember?" I strongly hoped I was correct in this interpretation. It was definitely to my advantage to have crazy Ben start shooting at someone else first as it afforded me time to run like hell.

She didn't say a word but slowly did a show and tell with an imaginary handgun that I associate with Clint Eastwood. "I have my own," she said, "It's bigger than yours, and, I know how to use it, and it's right in *this* bag."

With that she laid out several different types of bullets on the table in front of me. Each had its own lethal characteristics, and, she whispered, "I have a different one in each cylinder."

"Wise move," I commented sagely.

"We can go now," she said. "Don't forget the briefcase."

There followed a perfect week of sunshine and mimosas through the vineyards, shoreline and hills of northern California. Ben was briefly forgotten. To keep the chances of further blood-letting to a minimum, we returned from our wanderings directly to the airport in time for my departure for Paris. We arrived rather early and sat there over a couple of fruit juices. In fact, I had grown very fond of Julia, despite her homicidal proclivities. This was turning into a tearful farewell.

"Look," I confessed, "I am not very good at these farewell things. Why don't we say goodbye now. It has been a wonderful holiday, even though it started out strangely. But on the other hand, I feel like I have had the total California experience, so thanks. It was great. Really, I mean that. But what about you, what are you going to do now?"

"Oh, I called in this morning, and they have taken Ben into custody; so for the moment, I am safe."

Much relieved at the turn of events, I stood up, and we had a weepy sort of goodbye. Then I turned and headed off briskly to the departure lounge and she toward the car park.

I had gone maybe halfway down the corridor when I heard the sound of someone closing on me fast. "Oh my God, Ben!" I thought. I turned round, but it was Julia – who grabbed me, hugged me close and pressed me up against the wall in a compromising position. I had no idea I still had that sort of charm. She nibbled my ear, until I realised she was actually whispering.

"The gun. It's still in your case."

"Oh my God." I had completely forgotten.

"Give me the briefcase," she whispered, and I slipped it to her. She vanished into the Ladies' Room. Two minutes later she handed it to me, considerably lighter.

"That was close," she said, waved, and retreated, heavily armed, toward the car park.

11

The hypnotic briefcase

Paris, 1983

THE REASON I had flown halfway around the world from the island of Fiji to Paris was attend a conference at UNESCO. I had been housed in a rather plush hotel in the centre. I had lived there in 1978/79 and still had many friends in the city. Among these were a diminutive, rather mystical, Lebanese man and his much larger Jamaican wife, who always extended the hand of friendship whenever I was around. On this occasion, the mystical element was to save my bacon in a very peculiar way.

Just after the conference ended, I made a trip by train out to another friend in Viroflay. I went there straight from the UNESCO office, which meant that I was encumbered by a rather heavy briefcase stuffed with papers, including my travel documents. Rather than haul it around France with me, I decided to consign the case to a locker in the railway station just before leaving for my day out. I did this, was given a chunky key bearing the number of the locker, and took off in haste to make the next train.

The day was sunny and relaxing and I made my way back as the sun was setting, and went to collect my briefcase from its steel home. That was when I discovered that my key had left my presence and was nowhere to be found. Panic ensued, as I was due to fly out the following morning from Charles de Gaulle Airport. The custodian of the lockers explained to me that there was precisely nothing he could do, despite my obvious deteriorating mental state.

I hastened round to the Lebanese friend with my tale of woe and impending catastrophe, and he listened dispassionately as I advanced into a higher level of panic.

"We shall find it, I will show you," he assured me, though I could not imagine how this was to be achieved.

He took me the railway station, following a slow process of disengaging his car from the two that had wedged him in, bumper to bumper. This he did in the very French way of nudging them backwards and forwards; a process made less damaging by the rubber bumpers that seem to be standard on French cars – probably for this very reason. It certainly allowed Parisians to fit more cars into the average street than would otherwise be possible. It seemed to symbolise the Gallic indifference to property, rather than, say, the Teutonic view of the sanctity of it. Soon we were on our way, with him combining a Middle Eastern and French creative way of negotiating traffic that had me clinging to the seat belt. I was already far from relaxed before we started, and the anxiety was building with each motored moment.

Eventually, after more creative parking, we entered the station and made for the left luggage office. There, my

Lebanese friend, Walid, engaged the clerk in a long and detailed examination of the rules and regulations regarding the recovery of the contents of the lockers.

"OK," he said, turning in my direction. "What is the number of your locker?" This was a bombshell, because at that moment I realised that I had not memorised the key number and had no idea what it was. I explained that, now even more crestfallen than before.

"That makes it more difficult – but not impossible," Walid noted, with less confidence than he had displayed before. So he returned to the clerk, and an even longer discussion ensued, with Walid making notes very carefully in a small, leather-covered notebook. He then read back the conclusions to the clerk, and proceeded to explain something that took the official by surprise. I heard the bureaucrat say, "Well, yes, it's possible – if you could make such a thing happen."

Walid regained some of his assurance, turned to me and explained that if I could give a detailed description, first, of the exact contents of the locker, and show some proof that the item was mine – like something with a name that matched my ID, then the clerk would release the case to me.

"Once you identify the locker, the clerk will open it, and if everything matches, you are on your way."

This seemed perfectly reasonable to me, except for one thing: how was I to identify the locker without the key number? Walid's answer to this was to suggest that we walk around, and try to get a sense of where I had put the briefcase. There were hundreds of lockers, but off we went – and it soon became clear to me that I had no idea where the locker was situated among the rows and rows of identical steel boxes.

Back to the counter and further negotiations, after which Walid was able to inform me that the clerk could not open an indefinite number of these containers, and that we basically had one shot at it, and maybe the lockers on either side, and that was it. Otherwise we, and the official, would be here all night. At this point, the situation seemed to be without a practical solution, given my poor memory and the firmness of French bureaucracy. (It is, after all, a French word.)

Walid, however, did not seem to be resigned to failure – far from it.

"Now, this is what we are going to do," he explained in a very matter-of-fact way. "You see, despite your feeling that you do not, you *do* actually know which locker it is in which you put the briefcase, but that is itself locked into your subconscious memory where you cannot easily access it in the normal way. What we have to do is dig down and find that memory by tricking your brain." I had no idea what he was talking about, and even less about how he thought he was going to make this happen. But on the other hand, I *was* desperate.

"Now, I want you to say to yourself, silently, 'I am going to find my briefcase. I *do* know where it is.' Say it about six times, like you mean it. Then I want you to think of something else entirely."

My look must have conveyed my total amazement at what he was suggesting.

"No, trust me: it will work," he reassured me.

"But, what then?" I enquired.

"Then you will take off and run up and down the locker rows fast. Do *not* think about the briefcase. Then we shall see what will happen." It was that last part that intrigued me because I had visions of lightning striking, or some apparition appearing. I mean, what was going to stop my mad dash up and down the rows? He was not forthcoming on that matter at all. I had the distinct impression that he didn't actually know, and anyway, this whole thing seemed insane. Walid was, I knew, a great believer in the mystical properties of pyramids, the Bermuda Triangle and such, and had expounded at length on these things over several dinners. Was it a Lebanese thing? I wondered.

Walid explained his proposal to the astonished clerk, who admitted that it didn't contravene any known rules, though he wasn't going to be responsible if my careering around the left luggage centre resulted in any bodily injury to me. But I could see that he was intrigued by the curious nature of Walid's proposal.

"Can you imagine the odds against this working, when I have several hundred lockers in here, all identical?" the official asked, between puffs on a large pipe.

"Right, let's start with this row," said Walid, "then when you come to the end, don't think about where you go next, just follow your instincts. Keep thinking about something else, and keep the pace swift." He led me to a row in the middle, followed by the clerk, now thoroughly caught up in the oddity of the whole thing. Walid pointed me straight up a row, and said, "Are you ready, and saying to yourself that you will find the case?"

I confirmed that I was, having intoned the mantra very confidently to myself.

"Now think about some other situation or problem, right?" he told me, and I did. With that, he pushed me and I started off up the row at a reckless pace, and when I reached the end I just kept going down a row some distance away, and so on, never allowing myself to think about what I was doing.

By now a small crowd had gathered around the blue haze of the clerk and his pipe, watching in confusion as this fellow dashed up and down the rows, seemingly in some sort of trance. They asked the clerk what was happening, and he told them – so Walid informed me later – that this was an experimental way of locating lost property.

"Is it like dowsing?" one of the passengers asked.

"I have no idea what it is like," the clerk assured them. "Plus, it hasn't worked yet," he added, imposing a true Gallic sense of scepticism.

I don't know how many rows I had roared up and down, because my mind was resolutely fixed elsewhere – when suddenly I wasn't running any more. This was astonishing, because nothing had caught my notice. I had simply stopped. There was a locker to my left and one to my right. Actually, there were four because there were two in each unit, one above the other. But I did remember that I had reached *up* to insert the briefcase, and so the lower ones were eliminated.

"Don't move," came a familiar voice from far off, because they had heard me stop. "Stay exactly where you are."

After a few seconds a small crowd began to approach, heralded before their arrival by clouds of blue cigarette smoke, like some distant locomotive. Up the row they came, the clerk already brandishing a ring of keys.

"Which side?" he enquired. My left arm shot up, and my hand was firmly planted on the door to one locker. "Are you sure?" he asked me. "Because you don't get too many chances." Of course, I was *not* sure at all because I had no idea what process had brought me here.

Walid intervened, saying, "Oh, he cannot be sure, because he is now back to using the other part of his brain, which is totally confused by the whole thing."

"Like me," said the clerk, and he approached and peered at the number on the lock. From his chain he selected one key and with a flourish inserted it as the other passengers crowded around to see the conclusion to this charade.

One of them asked, "What is supposed to be inside?" I told them and the clerk slowly and surreptitiously opened the door to reveal...

A black briefcase.

Before I was allowed to touch it, he asked me what he would find inside. I told him that, among other papers, there would be an airline ticket to the Fiji Islands with my name on it. I took out my passport and gave it to him so he could compare the details. Now the crowd squeezed as close as possible, and the clerk, fully aware of his central role in this unfolding drama, clicked open the locks and *very slowly* raised the lid. He leaned forward to conceal his actions, and thereby heighten the drama, and then turned round with a flourish holding an airline ticket.

There was a collective gasp from everyone – except me, because I had already recognised the briefcase and had been plunged into shock earlier, and of course, Walid, who looked totally unsurprised, but happy that I had been released from my curse. The clerk asked me why I had stopped, and I confessed that I had no more idea than he did.

He handed me the briefcase and shook my hand.

"I have been working here for almost thirty years," he said to the crowd in general, which had applauded briefly. "And, let me tell you, I have never seen anything like that." I was pretty sure he had not.

"Well, remember it, and maybe you can use the method in the future, and perhaps become famous," responded Walid. Several among the crowd slapped me on the back and said it had all been fantastic.

Clutching the briefcase, I directed Walid into a bistro to recover from the exertions and tension of the last half-hour.

"How on earth did you know about that routine?" I asked him. Stirring his Turkish coffee, he surprised me in a way I certainly never anticipated.

"I didn't," he said. "It just seemed like a good idea, and there was nothing else we could do."

"But it worked!" I said in surprise.

"Yes, isn't that amazing? he replied, and downed the coffee in one. "Just don't lose it again."

12

Typhoons, lettuce and temporal displacement

NEW ZEALAND, 1983 (OR WAS IT 1944?)

1983 WAS A good year to end up in New Zealand. Possibly you did? Several unsuspecting people who never intended to go there did indeed end up there. I was one. However, sort of anticipating me was an American businessman who was flying home from Los Angeles to northern California. He heard his flight called earlier than he had expected, and with a gate change that required some athletic manoeuvring on his part. He dashed to another part of the airport, where the ground staff snatched his ticket and he disappeared down the boarding tunnel just as the door was closing. Of course, nothing as impromptu would *ever* happen in these security-conscious days.

The plane had been in the air for a little while when the captain came on the tannoy, welcoming everyone aboard and confirming the destination. He then added that the flying time would be somewhere around 20 hours and they would be stopping in Fiji. This is not a normal route for the San Francisco area, and so the next time the passenger saw a member of the cabin crew, he asked her:

"Why are we taking such a roundabout route to Oakland?"

"We are not going to Oakland, sir. We are going to Auckland," she replied.

The flight attendant was then subjected to a serious crisis of confidence when he asked, "Auckland, where is that?"

"Let me give you a clue, sir," she said. "This plane belongs to Air New Zealand."

After a few moments of cardiac arrest, he remembered enough geography to realise that New Zealand was on the other side of the world, wasn't it? Indeed it was, and there was nothing he, or anyone else, could do about it now. The captain arranged to send a message to his family that he would be delayed on business, and in all fairness Air NZ never charged him for his mistake, in addition to showing him more movies than he knew existed and stuffing him full of food. Plus, he got to stop over in Fiji – twice – once out, once back. He was such a devoted family man that he flew straight back on the plane's return trip to LA.

I often wondered which of many great lines he used on his return, when his wife asked him, "What delayed you?" Perhaps imagining some shady tryst.

"I had to go to Fiji twice," would have been my answer, for no-one but a fool would try to deceive his wife with a story as ridiculous as that. Anyway, the *Fiji Times* ran an article on him, including photographs, and so his alibi was watertight.

I mention this to convince you that New Zealand, generally thought of as a rather stolid and conservative place, situated to the right and down a bit from Australia, is actually capable of a few surprises, and, of course, is the location for many of the mega-movies of today, such as *Lord of the Rings*.

My own very brief and unintended conjunction with New Zealand occurred when I was returning to my post as a government advisor in the Fiji Islands. This followed a visit to the USA and Paris that had, as the previous two chapters have revealed, yielded some odd excitement of their own. In my case, I was scheduled to go back to work in Fiji but ended up in New Zealand, unlike our friend earlier who ended up in both Fiji and New Zealand, never intending to go to either.

The reason for my visit to the Kiwis was the result of something that all too often wreaks havoc with travel plans in that part of the world: a cyclone (or hurricane, or typhoon, take your pick). After the long flight from LA, broken only by a short stopover in Hawaii, our flight approached that south-west corner of the South Pacific where the 300+ constituent members of the Fiji Islands are located. Normally my flight would terminate at the diminutive national airport located at Nadi on the western side of the main island of Viti Levu.

Between our flight and that objective stood the formidable presence of Hurricane Oscar, and since all cyclones seemed to strike with full force on the *western* side of the country, where the airport was located, the potential for air traffic disruption was maximised. This is especially true when you realise that Suva, the country's capital on the eastern side, is as far from Nadi as you can be on Fiji's main island – but there was no time to move the airport now.

Our captain came on the tannoy to tell us that Fiji Air Traffic Control, whose employees were at that moment hanging onto anything solid they could lay their hands on, was warning us not to attempt a landing. So, "in the interest of safety", the captain told us, he would be flying straight through to Auckland, on New Zealand's North Island. I happened to know that Air NZ *refuelled* in Nadi, so this was not good news, and I wondered whether we should not take our chances with 200 km/hour winds, rather than drop in silence, the fuel tanks exhausted, 35,000 feet into the shark-infested waters of the South Pacific. The captain, who clearly also majored in ESP, immediately stated that this new destination was well within our fuel supplies. I could not, of course, see whether he was crossing his fingers when he said that.

There is, I confess, a certain excitement in getting to see a country you didn't have a clue you were even visiting ten minutes before. No-one in Nadi was going to be gnashing their teeth or tearing their hair because I did not arrive. They had other things on their mind, like not joining us at 35,000 feet without an aeroplane. And so we bade farewell to Fiji, represented below us by the edge of a roaring swirl of angry air, and took off for a little corner of Britain in the Antipodes.

Upon landing at Auckland, we were told that we would be accommodated very comfortably at a hotel – at the airline's expense, of course – "until other arrangements could be made." Our 'Fiji refugee' group was relatively small because Auckland had been the ultimate destination of the flight, and only a few of the passengers had intended to disembark in what was left of Nadi. But there were other folks here in the hotel already, from different flights also heading for Fiji, who had been stranded. This was clearly 'Fiji Central' for Air NZ.

My only concern had been that I was going to miss a business meeting with a young woman who was flying out from London to meet me in Fiji. I need not have worried. There she was sitting next to me at dinner that evening, similarly stranded, so now I even had a companion.

As everyone knows, I am sure, travel information of any sort is classified under the Official Secrets Act, because it is harder than pulling teeth to squeeze it out of the representatives of the sinking ship, plunging aircraft or, worst of all, airport counter staff who, surrounded by computers, faxes and, in those days, telex machines, seem to be at the centre of some gigantic

133

information void. "No, sir, I cannot confirm whether we have any planes left, or whether the flight to the Bongo Islands was seized by aliens."

Anyone having any doubts about this should read an account of how Pan Am handled the flow, or rather non-flow, of information to desperate relatives for days in a bid to control liability after the destruction of Flight 103 over Lockerbie. To a large extent, they brought about their own extinction by this uncaring manipulation of tortured people. I am not saying for a moment that Air NZ was behaving like this. The simple fact was that they, along with the rest of the world, did not know (a) how long Hurricane Oscar would hang around, and (b) how much of the airport it would leave behind. But they did say they would take us to our intended destination "at the first possible moment". For that to happen, they also told us to "stay in the hotel". By day three, this was becoming ridiculous. But I am jumping ahead.

Having now found a companion, I did not feel quite so stranded, and since she had now interviewed me, she could in all conscience continue to Fiji and hit the beaches. But we were rather beginning to feel entombed by the end of Day 2. I fancied we would be scratching lines in the wall soon to keep a record of the days.

It wasn't all tedium. There was, for instance, the rather florid but very charming gentleman who introduced himself, I believe, as "Webb's Wonderful Lettuce". I am not sure how he had ended up there, but he was clearly king of the British lettuce market. Incidentally, the British really didn't discover lettuce until the 1970s, and Mr Webb had a lot to do with that. Lettuce, however, is a rather limited topic of conversation, especially as, at that time, I didn't eat it. The British lady who was now my companion was, nonetheless, mightily impressed at meeting Mr Webb.

"It's like meeting Mr Hoover," she said.

"What an odd choice," I said. "The Thirty-First President was not exactly dynamite – few engineers are."

She looked puzzled, frowned, and then said, "Not *Herbert* Hoover – Mr Hoover, the inventor of the vacuum cleaner."

"Ah, I see – household name you mean, like Thomas Crapper."

But, being the pretentious, trivia-laden busybody I have always been, I could not let this go without adding, "He didn't, you know."

The effect was lost when she said, "Who didn't do what?"

"Hoover. He didn't invent the vacuum cleaner. It was invented by an Ohio janitor called Murray Spangler, who suffered from asthma, and wanted to keep the dust down." I gave her one of my Oliver Hardy looks – the one that he saved for the moment he smugly wiggled his attenuated tie with his fingers.

"So, why don't we call it a Spangler then?" she enquired, very logically.

"Because he sold the patent to 'Boss' Hoover, in Canton, Ohio, who went on to invent the franchise system, and make a ton of money."

"Oh, I see," she said with a puckered brow. "What has this got to do with lettuce?"

"Nothing, but it has a lot to do with getting out of this hotel. We are both going nuts. Let's find some place to go."

The good folks from the airlines were not at all keen on this breakdown in the herd structure. They warned us that if a flight should take off while we were away gallivanting, then on our head be it. By this point gallivanting definitely beat a run of sevens and any runaway flights that Air NZ might let slip through the net.

But, the question was, where to go? Clearly we didn't want to go far, because we were a little bit intimidated by the airline representative's 'take it or leave it' statement. We decided to go down to the bus station, see what was going where, and how long the round trip would take.

Finally at liberty, we breathed the clean air of freedom and strolled through the streets of Auckland heading for the bus station. Everything had a curiously familiar and comforting look to it, because it seemed like the UK I remembered from my schooldays. It was hard to say exactly in what way, but it was continuous 24-hour déjà vu. Still, we didn't linger in the stores because they were expensive in a way I had not seen since Abu Dhabi. And this place did not have oil.

At the bus station, that air of comfortable lassitude continued to prevail, and we were soon in deep conversation with a bus driver, complete with his mug of tea and a tabloid. We explained our predicament, including the fact we did not wish to become unintentional immigrants who missed the plane, even though it looked like a pleasant enough place.

"Well, my little orphans of the storm," he began, "you could not do better than to accompany me on my run to North Shore. You will get to see a bit of Auckland and the suburbs, and then, at the end you can have a stroll on the beach, breathe in the ocean air, and return refreshed two hours later when I pick you up. What do you think of that?"

"Outstanding," we replied, and gave him the fare, whereupon he told us to make ourselves comfy in the bus.

Slowly it started to fill, and then we were off. It really was the suburbia of my youth. This picture was strongly reinforced when schoolchildren entered kitted out *exactly* as I had been in the 50s.

"Hard to believe that straight south from here is the Antarctic," I observed.

"Heavens, yes," my companion replied. "My first thought would be Calais or Dieppe." It was a very odd feeling, like someone had towed the UK here in the depths of night.

Before long, the bus came to a shady turn-around, and our new friend told us to "hop out", remember the spot and be back here "on the dot".

"Or what?" I asked, meaning was his the last bus.

"I will fly off to Fiji without you," he commented. Then he started the bus and left, chuckling.

The first thing we observed about our destination was that there was absolutely *no one* around. But we could tell where the sea was, and made our way toward it. It really was extraordinarily quiet. Ahead of us was a café and ice-cream kiosk of the type I remembered from my pre-teen holidays in Tenby in Wales. However, there was nobody around. What followed was the strangest experience of my life without question, and I will tell you right now, up front, I have absolutely *no explanation* for what happened. So don't ask.

"Look at that," I said to my lady friend, pointing at the little car park beside the café.

"What's there?" she enquired, seeing nothing strange.

"The cars. There's not one of them made after the war, and some of them are in great shape. There's an Austin 7, and there's a Morris from the twenties. There must be some sort of rally, but usually the people stay with their cars, otherwise you have grubby hands all over them, and collectors are paranoid about that."

We looked over some of the vehicles, and decided it had to be some sort of organised rally as there were no modern cars parked here.

We strolled onto the beach and it was so English. A couple of people sat in those folding canvas deckchairs that left an entire generation of Brits without the end of a finger or two. There were a couple of people in uniform, though again that was the heavy uniform material that I remembered from a Britain full of about-to-be-demobilised soldiers just after the war.

"Those old wartime fortifications over there, you'd think they would have torn them down. They are so ugly on this lovely bay, and there's even some barbed wire. How long has it been?" she pondered.

"Forty years," I replied. "They certainly are in good shape, and you can almost imagine the folks inside watching out for the Japanese."

"Well, that certainly fits the picture," she said, pointing at a couple walking a dog along the beach. They were wearing matching tweed outfits, and the man was actually wearing, and this was a first for me, knickerbockers.

"Good grief, is someone making a film here or what?" she asked.

We watched them stroll, and leave toward the car park. It was all beginning to feel very odd.

"Is it time to head for the bus?" she asked, looking out at the sea after we had been sitting on the beach.

"I suppose we could make a leisurely stroll back. He will be here in about twenty minutes. I would hate him to take off without us."

On the way back she asked me, "Did you fly across the Dateline to get here? Coming from London I did not. So you probably gained a day. What happens when I go to Fiji?"

I reassured her that despite her long journey, and the continuation to Fiji, she would remain within the same calendar because the International Dateline had been 'bent' to go around Fiji to the east, even though it should go bang through the middle of the island of Taveuni. Of course I had crossed it, and lost a day, coming from Los Angeles.

"So what day is it for you?" she enquired.

I had owned for some time a fine piece of electronic wizardry that could tell you the time, day, year, and month on LCD readout. It also had an alarm. So, to answer her question (because, I admit, I was getting confused now), pushing the button to display the date, I said, "Ah, it's still showing Tuesday, instead of Wednesday. I will need to reset...."

"What is it?" she asked, for I had stopped dead in my tracks.

"The year. It says 1944. The year I was born. Look."

"Good God, so it does," she exclaimed in surprise. "Why would it do that?"

Completely baffled and at a loss, I said, "Why would they have 1944 on a watch they made in 1982? That is absurd. It is also very creepy."

But there it was, and nothing I could do would make it go away. The day and the month were correct – well, as I had observed, the day was wrong because I had not reset it after crossing the Dateline. I felt distinctly uncomfortable. We were at that point at the place where the beach exited into the shady area near the bus stop.

"But it would explain," she said, with a rather forced laugh, "why all those old cars were here, and in such good shape."

"What old cars?" I asked sweeping my arm around. There in the car park were two Toyotas and a Honda Civic.

"There's the bus!" she said, waving to the driver, who was waving back. I was now totally confused.

"How was it?" he enquired as, with a hiss of air, the mechanical door opened to let us in.

"At least the Japanese didn't land," she replied.

"What Japanese?" he asked, confused.

"Oh, just a figure of speech," I interjected. "Hondas, Toyotas and the like."

"Oh," he said, still puzzled.

Once the bus was underway, we started talking about the two Edwardian English schoolteachers who swore they had walked into the epoch of Marie Antoinette in the gardens of Versailles. Though they were ladies of impeccable reputation, the public at large, while intrigued, considered them, ultimately, to be barmy.[21]

"I don't suppose we should say anything about this," she commented, "Though I hope your watch doesn't get stuck in that position. Still, as you say, why would you put a facility for an old date on a modern watch? Seems redundant doesn't it? Do you think you can fix it?"

"I don't know," I answered. "I am not even sure exactly how it works. The man in the shop set it for me, and it has kept perfect time and date until now." I prepared to fiddle with it.

21 On August 10th, 1901 Charlotte Anne Moberly, principal of St Hugh's College, Oxford, and her friend Dr Eleanor Jourdain claimed to have experienced what they took to be some sort of time shift while walking through the gardens of Versailles, and claimed in a book they wrote in 1912 – An Adventure – to have briefly encountered a moment 109 years earlier, including a sight of Marie Antoinette.

"On the other hand..." I said, passing it to her.

"Well, Holy Moses," she exclaimed, for there, as clear as day, it said 1983.[22]

"Let's talk about lettuce," I said, and we drove back through the suburbs to our comfortable prison.

---

22 Casio told me that what had happened was "totally impossible".

13

On the banks of the mystic Nile

EGYPT, 1972 AND 1989

I saw a beauty of the Nile
Throwing stones at a crocodile
On the left-hand side of Egypt going in...
All sorts of things I saw
Things I'd never, never seen before
Lucky there was nobody about.[23]

---

23 Lancashire comedian George Formby made this unlikely song popular
during the Second World War.

I HAD BEEN to Egypt before the visit that is the main subject of this chapter. In fact, Egypt had been, without doubt, the place in the entire world that I wanted to visit most. Maybe it was all the Bible stories, Cleopatra – receiving a boost from Liz Taylor during my adolescence – those immortal pyramids, the Battle of the Nile, and the fact that I had believed that all my classmates and I were going to be vaporised as a consequence of the Suez fiasco of 1956, when imperialists old and new tried out the old ways to challenge the impudence of Nasser in claiming the Suez Canal as his own. The Americans soon put paid to that folly, and Egypt got back what the British stole from the French, who got it from the Turks, who had suzerainty over the Egyptians. Anyway, it had always been there – Egypt, I mean – in the background all through my life. It was one of the *magical* words, like Zanzibar, the Sanjak of Novi Pazar, the Pitcairn Islands, or Tonga.

My first visit was during the time of Gamal Abdel Nasser, the impossibly handsome, popular, and frustratingly successful nemesis of the West. That is not strictly true, for Nasser had died the previous year, in 1970, and the nation was still in a state of shock. I flew over from Jeddah, across the Red Sea, to spend some 'local leave'. The definition of local leave in Saudi Arabia was that you had to go somewhere that had at least as rotten a climate as Jeddah. Jeddah itself always had the miasmic air of a recently drained fishpond. Cairo's air was at least drier and more bearable.

Without any specific reason, I booked myself into the Semiramis Hotel, or what you now have to call the *Old* Semiramis Hotel, because what replaced it was entirely featureless. But the *Old* Queen of the Nile, as it was familiarly known, was one of the great hotels of an era, already fast becoming a memory. It belonged to a world of steamboats, Agatha Christie, and Imperial Airways landing its seaplanes on Mother Nile, topped off by a slightly zany monarchy, and somewhere in the background, pulling the strings, the British. Cairo had then, and still has, a pervasive, almost palpable, sense of conspiracy and stratagem – not on an individual basis, for the people are raffishly wonderful – but more or less just lurking, Ottoman-like, in the air. The whole place *looks* like it was built for intrigue. Whatever the truth, the fact is that Egypt has had longer to practise and refine its wiles than almost any place other than China.

Appropriate to its crucial place as the crossroads from the Middle East to North Africa, and – via the Suez Canal – from Imperial Britain to Imperial India, Egypt boasted hotels on a grand scale, the stuff of many an espionage page-turner. In its way, Cairo was the Constantinople of the south – a strategic corridor between West and East, ancient beyond words, filled with colourful and exotic minorities of Levantines, Jews, Armenians, and Greeks – and most important, both locations commanding a narrow waterway of global strategic importance.

I have to admit that when I pulled up in the cab in front of the Semiramis, I had mixed feelings. On the plus side, it was bang on the Nile, and had been the first major Cairo hotel to secure such a location. So great views from the right rooms were assured, even if the right rooms were not. On the negative side, the place looked run down. There were two reasons for this: one I knew, the other I am glad I did not. The first was that during the Nasser years, tourism had declined badly. It would be more correct to say that *profitable* tourism had fled, and what had taken its place was an influx of citizens from the Socialist Bloc. After Nasser had been more or less driven into the arms of the Russians by the phobic times of the 'Red Scare', the Soviets stepped into the gap and took on the responsibility of building the huge Aswan Dam that the World Bank had fudged as a result of American pressure. America was about to display the same level of counterproductive foreign policy to the other demon of those times – Fidel.

So when I got to Egypt, the tourist industry was in the Egyptian equivalent of the Great Depression. The second reason why the Semiramis looked the worse for wear was that soon after my departure, they were going to be pulling the whole edifice down. Shepheard's, the other, better-known hotel, had already gone as the result of an arsonist's torch during a political demonstration. It had been replaced by an anonymous modern structure that totally belied the name, which it retained, leading to disappointment for thousands of tourists who were seeking out the legendary hotel.

When the Semiramis had opened in 1907, its location was everything one might hope for. Not only was it on the Nile's east bank, but also it was between the home of the Walda Pasha (the mother of the Khedive, or ruler), and the home of her daughter, Princess Nimet Kamal-el-Dine; exceptional neighbours. The original owners of this solidly respectable piece of real estate were the splendidly named Société Suisse Egyptienne des Hotels en Egypte. As with many palatial buildings in remote and exotic places at that time, the architect was Italian, the contractors Belgian. Despite the Italian conception, the child was decked out as a Frenchman with gilded mirrors, Louis XVI furniture, Gobelin tapestries, and salons.

Carried away by the Babylonian associations (Semiramis was a queen of the Assyrians), this hotel boasted the first and only roof garden, as a gesture to the Hanging Gardens of Babylon. This afforded whatever cooling breezes came off the Nile, and an unsurpassed view of the Pyramids before the suburbs gobbled them up. This garden became *the* place to be seen in the evening, or over tea as the enervating vapours of the Cairo day yielded to evening – which came a little earlier at that altitude. It was here, in 1956, that the Aga Khan was weighed in precious metals for the last time. After 71 years in office, he died the following year.

Inside the Semiramis it was evident that time had stopped. Even the air seemed antique. I had the distinct impression that as I opened the door, a series of functionaries around the building were slowly activated from a sleep akin to that of the folks entombed in the Valley of the Kings, like an old gramophone record was being started up with the needle on the record. The grandness of the place was engaged in a fatal battle with neglect, penury, and an uncomfortable marriage of convenience with socialism. When later I was to read Stephen King's *The Shining*, I could always imagine those resurrected visions occurring in the cavernous corridors of Egypt's equivalent of the *Overlook*. I always expected my surroundings to morph through some time warp and lean, swarthy Levantines in frock coats, decorations and the fez to appear; walking, *conspiratorially* of course, along the corridor ahead of me, trailing a pungent blue haze of rich Turkish tobacco from delicately held cigarettes. I never actually experienced it, though, as it would have taken a precise level of mental dislocation that I could never *quite* achieve.

En route to the reception desk, I caught my reflection in several signs; all of them, of course, in French – *la langue internationale* of the time – inscribed in deeply recessed copper plate on burnished brass, with that glorious warm patina only decades of elbow-grease can achieve. Before I reached the desk, I passed a large framed engraving over the fireplace dedicated to *Napoléon en Egypte*. The owners, being Swiss and, supposedly neutral, could get away with this bit of *lèse-majesté* that rather poked a finger in the eye of the British officers who frequented the bar there and would surely recall that it was Nelson who put an end to Napoleon's adventure in Egypt. It says something of those times that it survived.

I found it necessary to put a high premium on antiquity, historical associations and ambience, because, frankly speaking, socialism had done a number on everything else. The rooms were *huge*, with two sets of grand double doors to enter in style. The beds, which were the only British furnishings in the entire place, were sagging rather by now; but who cares – I would not have missed this place for anything, especially as her days were numbered. The attendants were still dressed in the elaborate uniform of the *dragoman*, and the one allocated to my well-being always addressed me as *"Effendi"*.[24] The Ottoman Empire was back. Like everyone in this establishment, he operated at one pace only: regally measured and deliberate – all very appropriate to these settings.

I knew it would be a shock to step out from this life-in-aspic, shadowy world into the bright sunshine and realities of teeming Cairo. I was not prepared for what a change there would be. The thousands of Russians who had replaced the Western tourists had one real drawback for the local people: they had no money – well, no useful money, anyway. When I emerged from a surprisingly good, if not *grand*, breakfast complete in Poirot-style white-linen suit, I turned to my colleague, and made a brief remark to him *in English*. The effect was like detonating a mine in an Oxford lily pond – the transformation was instantaneous. The entire landscape came to life. One minute, nothing; the next moment there followed a period of relentless waving of merchandise that totally prevented us from going anywhere. I thought of those scenes in movies where a mob of people descend and the central figure disappears under the weight of the crush – his fate unseen, but clear. We were prevented from sharing this fate by the prompt arrival of the *dragoman*.

Return to the Nile

One of the rewards of being a professor is that occasionally a student remembers you in some way that is, itself, memorable. This occurred in 1988, when I received a call from the Embassy of Egypt in Washington, DC. The ambassador informed me

---

24 The *dragoman*, once an institution in Egypt, is virtually extinct now. The term meant an interpreter or guide working in Arabic, Turkish or Persian. But the name gathered more cachet when the embassies retained them and used them as couriers, decking them out in ever-more fantastic uniforms to outdo the other embassies. My main reason for loving this word is that it takes the plural form *dragomans*.

that I had been invited to go to Egypt as the guest of the Speaker of the National Assembly. This was a direct result of the fact that, just before this call, one of my doctoral students had graduated – and he was the son of the Speaker of the National Assembly. It was all very correct; it would have been rather compromising if I had received such a request *before* he had graduated. Soon the formal invitation on the letterhead of the National Assembly arrived, and I notified the Ambassador of a suitable time for my travel. And so I departed for a very memorable and surprising week.

My flight had been arranged on Egypt Air, but due to an error on my part I was issued with a tourist class ticket, whereas the authorisation was for first class. Still, the flight was very pleasant. The couple sitting next to me were from the Midwest, and they asked me whether I was in their 'group'. I had no idea what group that was, but I told them no, that I was travelling alone. In answer to further questions, I told them that I was going as a guest of the National Assembly, and I am not sure they believed me.

Once we had landed at Cairo and taxied to the point of disembarkation, there was a message from the Captain.

"Would everyone remain in their seats? If there is a Dr Randall Baker among the passengers, would he please make himself known to the cabin staff?"

I stood up, and two of the stewardesses came toward me. But behind them came a gentleman in a black morning suit, sporting white gloves, who in turn was followed by two well-appointed military officers. I think most people imagined that a well-organised terrorist threat had been foiled. However, the gentleman in black announced himself as the *Chef du Protocole*, shook my hand, and the two military types saluted. At least I was now vindicated in the eyes of my travelling companions. The welcome party led me off the plane, into a black limousine and sped me to the VIP lounge, where we discovered my luggage had not made it onto the plane. I did not see it for another four days, which was awkward because it contained all the gifts for the people I was going to meet.

The airline provided an emergency kit, and their apologies were fulsome, as this somewhat took the edge off my resplendent welcome. At that point, the *Chef du Protocole* introduced me to a small but stocky man called Ali.

"Ali is your guide and your bodyguard, and will be with you at all times. I have here your schedule, and you must feel free to make any amendments you wish, plus whatever you wish to see; we shall be delighted to accommodate you."

Ali smiled, and shook hands with an iron grip. I studied the schedule, and it certainly covered nearly all the bases, including a visit to Abu Simbel on the Upper Nile. I explained that I had been to Egypt before, and rather than duplicate my earlier visit, I would like to take out the main attractions, like the Pyramids, and add a few that I had failed to catch. Ali, as always, said "No problem".

We made it to the hotel rather late, and Ali informed me he had the next room. I told him, jokingly, that I thought bodyguards always stayed outside the door at night.

"Oh, no," he informed me. "If I fell asleep there they would see me and shoot me. Better I come rushing out of my room at the right moment."

It made sense to me. Then we got on to the topic of the next day. I noticed that I was to go to the National Assembly to be greeted by the speaker, Rifaat el-Mahgoub, and shown around. A thought suddenly popped into my mind:

"Ali, what am I going to wear?"

"That is what my wife usually asks me," he commented.

"No, I have no luggage – the only clothes I have are the ones I am in now. I have been wearing these continually for two days. What shall I do?"

Ali looked challenged. He told me the shops were probably closed now, but he had some shirts, so let's try one. I had a good eight inches on Ali vertically, and I hate to think what horizontally. He returned from his room with a grey shirt, and

I tried it. It was a tribute to his excellent musculature that, despite his diminutive size, I was able to get into it at all. I felt, rather appropriately, like a mummy – as though I had been sewn into the garment.

"Look," he said, "you've got the suit, which is the important thing, and if you keep the jacket closed, then they will not see the shirt. Are you having trouble breathing?"

He asked this because the constriction around the neck was only just bearable. But, I told him, if it's just for a morning, I can survive – as long as we go immediately to the *suq* and find something my size.

"No problem."

The next morning I entered the limousine feeling like someone about to have a heart attack. As we descended at the Parliament Building, I noticed how the shirt improved my posture, because it would fly apart if I did not look like a major-general. Ali went round to open the door (I was not to get out on my own). He checked about him and we went into the National Assembly,[25] to a smart salute from the two guards.

Inside the building the predominant colour was not red, as in all other Parliaments I had visited, but green – the colour of Islam. There was the feeling of a very exclusive London club, betrayed only by numerous portraits of rotund gentlemen in fezzes. I was ushered into a well-appointed anteroom with an extraordinarily high ceiling to accommodate the vast chandelier. Various members of the Protocol Department kept me amused, until suddenly the doors opened and in came Dr el-Mahgoub.

I had met him once or twice before, and he belonged to a generation of Egyptians that is now, I believe, more or less extinct. The very cosmopolitan folks of Alexandria best exemplified them, and like them he was more comfortable

---

25 Now known as the People's Assembly.

in French than in English, and so we switched after the preliminaries. He was a natural gentleman, courtesy coming so instinctively to him that it was simply his manner at all times. I had not realised that the Assembly was in session, and so Dr el-Mahgoub was hard-pressed to find a few moments to escape.

He shook my hand, and holding my arm, thanked me very sincerely for everything I had done for his son. I reminded him that his son had done it himself, but that did not diminish the good doctor's gratitude. He told me that we would have a tour of the Assembly building, he would join me for a couple of meals, and we would meet some old friends who had also attended the Bloomington campus of Indiana University where I had my chair. I appreciated that he was caught up in the politics of the moment, and told him not to worry about me – nobody could be bored in Egypt.

"Yes," he said, "it is quite a responsibility being speaker in a country with the oldest legislature in the world. We have been making laws here for 6,000 years."

It was true in that case, as with many others, that the word 'old' simply acquires a totally different value in Egypt. This is especially true for someone who has lived in Indiana, which became a state in 1816. That was this morning by Egyptian standards. I mentioned this, and Dr el-Mahgoub told me, "You know, I was visiting a farm once, and it was producing an excellent crop of wheat and clover. I told the farmer, 'You really look after your land.' He told me, in reply, that he felt a duty to do so as it had been in cultivation for five thousand years! Can you imagine that?"

"You know, it took some of the farmers in Indiana less than 100 years to totally destroy the land, and now it is forest," I countered. "We could have done with some of your *alfallahin* over there."[26]

---

26 *Alfallahin* is the Egyptian term for 'peasants'.

We chatted over extremely strong Turkish coffee ("One of the better things they left us with," he commented), and then he had to return to business and so he asked one of the staff to show me around. I bade him goodbye, and thanked him profusely for this unique opportunity.

"It was my pleasure," he responded graciously. "And, by the way, you look just fine in Ali's shirt. No one would ever know." He vanished with a smile.

Well, I imagine the National Assembly still has some of the ways of the *suq*, and the tale had reached him. I am glad he said it as he left, not as he entered.

Our tour was fascinating, especially in its one-to-one format. Reflecting the doctor's words, there were many items from Pharaonic times stating, in hieroglyphs, the rights of the citizen vis-à-vis the ruler. There were laws in Greek (Alexandrian times), Latin (shades of Julius Caesar), Arabic, Turkish, French and English. The most prominent item, simply because of its size, was the state coach of King Farouk (himself of Albanian descent) that carried him from the Abdeen Palace to the Parliament.

"You see these papyri here," my guide indicated. "This is a legislative code, and it was written twice as long *before* the Roman Empire as we are after the Roman Empire."

This place, I thought, is a veritable time capsule. History begins here.

My visit over, the solemnity and dignity were cast aside as Ali and I made for the market to purchase the necessary items to replace those that were still in Airline Purgatory somewhere. In the land of the finest cotton, shirts were no problem – and fifteen years later, they are still as good as new. Ali suggested we walk a little, and then go back to the hotel so I could rest and we could go over the schedule. It was astonishingly hot, though the dry air made the heat more bearable.

In the café, we studied the schedule. I said to Ali, "You know, I have been to Egypt twice before, and my main aim was to see the treasures of Tutankhamun. The first time they

151

had gone to London, and the second time to Washington. So I never did get to see them. What about that? Is that something you can arrange?"

Ali returned a gesture of 'leave it to me', and went off to his room. Within a short time, he was back, and told me, "Get up early tomorrow, because we have to be at the Cairo Museum at 8 a.m."

Now that really was exciting news.

Promptly at 8 a.m., despite the worst the Cairene traffic could offer, we were on the doorstep. There was a small delegation to welcome us, and they ushered us inside. The vast place was totally empty, which was wonderful. We visited many well-known artefacts, but eventually made it to the spot where I wanted to be. This time there was no empty space with a note of apology. There it all was.

My guide was remarkably well-informed, and I was astonished to learn that some of the grains of wheat that had accompanied the young king into the tomb had actually been induced to sprout and grow recently. That is a quite astonishing living link with the Pharaohs. But the great moment came when we approached the sarcophagus of the king – something so very familiar as an image that it was hard to believe it really existed and was right in front of you.

They took down the barrier and I inspected it minutely; something crafted by people so long gone from this earth. There was something utterly compelling about this thought, like staring into a black hole of time.

The tour was totally absorbing, but for me the most intimate moment came when we entered the papyrus collection. My image of papyrus is of formalistic paintings, but of course it was also a medium for communication and storing information. My guide asked me what sort of thing I would like to see, for they had thousands.

"I would really like to see something very ordinary. I love Horus and Ra and Isis, but how about something from the everyday life of the people?"

He pulled open a huge drawer, and brought out a fragment of papyrus, part of its fibrous plant structure showing through. This document, however, was written in the demotic form, without the elaborate formalism of the sort of hieroglyphs we see on monuments. It looked very much like handwriting – which of course, it was. But still, it had an air of mystery because I could not read it. I asked my guide if he could.

"That is no problem, as the writing is rather clear," he commented, put on his glasses, and started, "Oh, this is a letter to some minor official and it says 'Please do something about our neighbours because they are wild and noisy and they keep us awake. We have to work and need to sleep.' Hmm, times don't change much do they?" he remarked, then looked at the next. "Ah, now this one is from a child, and the writing is a bit wild, but legible: 'Dear Father: You promised me that we would go to see the races and you forgot. I am upset.' Poor boy."

I wonder what that 'poor boy' would have thought as he penned that petulant note, if he'd known that people would be reading it 3,000 years after his death?

"I have often wondered," I asked the guide, "with respect to all these monumental buildings, how were they planned?"

At this, the guide walked over to another larger drawer, and pulled out of it a very substantial papyrus. He opened it in front of me, and it was the building plan for a temple. It took my breath away. The precision of the line, the extraordinary detail, and the explanations, finally revealed a level of sophistication that I should have appreciated simply from looking at the result, still standing all over the country. But this was magnificent.

The guide continued, "They had to have this level of precision beforehand because the blocks for these buildings were often quarried and shaped 600 miles from here. When they arrived, they were expected to fit. You cannot do that without plans."

"Unbelievable," was all I could say as I looked at the document in front of me. "And I suppose the result of these plans is standing somewhere out there?"

He looked closely and said, "Well, this is not one of the better preserved examples. Strange really, the stone edifice is largely eroded away, and yet the plans are still here as good as new. Useful if you want to rebuild, you see," he observed.

I had thought I was lucky to have a workshop manual for my 1977 Cadillac, but this was ridiculous.

My visit over, my head was reeling, and I wanted so earnestly to thank the guide.

"You are one of the best-informed guides I have ever encountered," I said by way of sincere praise.

"That is good news – though I am in fact, the Director of Antiquities for Egypt. But I am so glad you appreciated it all."

The faux pas seemed to slip by, and he left me unembarrassed.

Leaving the timeless shade of the Cairo Museum, and walking into the daylight was a physical jolt leaving you blinded and deafened as though you had been teleported to some other planet during rush hour. I was also aware of the hostile looks of a lot of sweaty Italians.

"What's wrong with them?" I asked Ali.

"Well, sir," he replied with a smile, "You were only supposed to be in there for an hour, but you were in for over two hours, and they were not allowed to go in until you came out."

A thousand Italian eyes looked daggers at me until the limo drove off into the maw of Cairo's traffic.

I was able to repeat the experience in the Valley of the Kings, where King Tut's tomb was firmly closed until the local Director of Antiquities (a very charming lady) and I had examined every word of the Book of the Dead, and communed with the environment where someone had lain undisturbed for so long.

The next major excitement for me was to be the journey to Abu Simbel, for which we had to go to Upper Egypt, and the twentieth-century creation of Lake Nasser that had threatened to destroy this ancient monument. Ali and I sat in the aircraft's First Class exchanging experiences, for we had really discovered a common identity and a wicked sense of irreverence. Nobody argued with him, I did notice that, which must have its benefits. But he was up for anything.

When we arrived in Abu Simbel by air, the Governor of Aswan Province was there to meet us. But best of all were the schoolgirls who lined our route, and sang a song of welcome. I could so easily get used to this. Remembering my Prince Charles bit, I stopped and chatted with a few, several of whom had some words of English. The Governor was a wonderful man with no pretensions, and a warm welcome. He had, in fact, been to Wales and told me he thought it a splendid little place, so we were off on the right foot. He knew I was a guest of the government, but not much more, I suspect.

Abu Simbel is one of the United Nations' great achievements. When the time came to build the Aswan Dam, there were a couple of consequences to be taken into account:

1. The Nile would no longer bring its load of silt from the highlands of Ethiopia and East Africa to replenish the fields. That was how the gentleman we heard of earlier was able to boast of farming a field that had produced for thousands of years. The inundation by the Nile brought mud, minerals, and organic matter that revitalised the soil every year. The dam would put paid to that, but it would also produce electricity that would be used to make fertilisers. Somehow, deep down, you knew this was *bad*.

2. Behind the dam was forming one of the biggest man-made lakes in the world. While much of the land to be inundated was pretty well barren, near the Nile course there were some of the finest monuments existing anywhere, carved from living rock.

To prevent the drowning of these monuments, UNESCO started a worldwide movement to save them. Eventually, they were raised in their entirety, with their living rock environment, onto a plateau above the flood level. Now it is hard to tell they were not always there. There they stand: vast, timeless, a little the worse for millennia of sandblasting, but awe-inspiring however you look at it. They stand amidst barren silence. But then, that is what they were supposed to do when Ramses II built the two temples, the larger one for himself, and the smaller for his wife Nefertari. His main object was to awe the Nubians with the power and majesty of the New Kingdom. They certainly must have done that, and they still do it today. Rounding out our group of four in the Land Rover was the very urbane and knowledgeable Director of Antiquities for these monuments.

When we arrived at the site of the two temples, carefully cut apart and numbered and then reassembled above the floodwater level between 1963 and 1968, it was hard to imagine that they had not always been here. Until, that is, you wander round behind them and see that this looks like something Cecil B DeMille might have organised, because the façade is just that. Behind it is a large, recent semicircular construction to contain the temples that also had to be extracted from the living rock. From the front, however, the effect was remarkable.

We listened in awe to the story of the construction of the temples (c.1250 BC), and I asked the Director why every second statue in Egypt was of Ramses II, or so it seemed to me, when this country had such an enormous history of dynasties. His answer could have been about a modern politician, not someone who died 3,000 years ago:

"First of all, Ramses ruled Egypt for 67 years, which is about three years longer than Queen Victoria's reign, and people did not, on average, live very long in those days. Then, he was a great believer in what we would call today the 'cult of personality' and made sure you could hardly turn a corner without seeing his image. Another point is that he wanted his image associated with all the works of the state – any temple, civic building, whatever. And, lastly, he was not above taking the statues of earlier pharaohs and altering the cartouche[27] to bear the hieroglyph of his name. Some things never change."

The Governor laughed and said, "Now, Ahmed, how many statues of President Mubarak do you see? And there is not even one of me. Maybe I should copy old Ramses and change one of the faces up there?" pointing at one of the *four* huge effigies of Ramses.

The Director laughed, and told the Governor that he would have him arrested for vandalism if he did that.

As had been the case at my other visits, there was nobody around, and the edifice stood warmed by the morning sun, which it faces. After touring the great temple, we wandered over to the smaller one, dedicated to the favourite wife. The Director pushed the door – it was locked. He excused himself and jogged off while we waited, watching the sun reflected in the waters of Lake Nasser.

He was back in a moment, and in his hand was a huge key in the shape of an Egyptian *ankh*. With a wave of his hand he ushered us to the door and offered me the mighty key. Once inside, we were able to see the traces of where the interior had been meticulously cut out of the rock, removed and reassembled. This has been expertly masked on the exterior. The director took us to the end of the long passageway, and pointed at a small niche. He explained:

"Now, bear in mind when this was built, the tools available and the sheer scale of this construction. Despite all that, the builders made it so that twice a year, at the solstices, the sun penetrates the entire length of the temple and illuminates the statues of Amon, Hamarkhis and the Pharaoh. This lasts only five minutes and then the light disappears. Even more incredible is that the God Ptah is never illuminated, for Ptah is the god of darkness."

---

27 The cartouche is the oval vertical shape that contains the name of the king, not unlike a Chinese seal. The oval stood atop a straight-line base, making the whole device look not unlike a bullet – hence the French name.

157

Having seen those architectural plans in the Cairo Museum, I had no doubt they had worked all that out in advance.

That evening, Ali and I rented the services of a *felucca*, or riverboat, still true to its timeless design with its versatile lateen sail, and we toured the islands of the Nile near our hotel. This was an experience we could have shared with anyone from the previous 5,000 years, and there are not too many of those. I asked Ali about his job in security, and whether that was a serious concern. He rolled his eyes, and said:

"It never stops. We have every sort of fanatic on earth here, plus we have strong tensions within the various parts of society – you know, the Copts,[28] the Palestinians, the Islamic extremists. It is difficult to keep up with them all. You cannot let down your guard for a moment, otherwise – well, you remember what happened to Sadat. There was an attack on a busload of tourists not so long ago, some fundamentalists wanting to drive the tourists away and cut the income from them. Then whatever we do with Israel is always wrong for somebody, and there are so many crazy people, and what can you do against people who actually want to die? But, it has been 5,000 years and we are still here, floating on the Nile."

That evening had been reserved for a folk music concert in a local theatre. We entered and the place was packed. Ali took me down to the front row, and looked concerned. He hastily waved over two unidentified men and got into a huddle with them. He looked concerned, and whispered, "Some prince from the Emirates is here and he and his wife are in our seats. Since he is royalty, there is not much we can do about it; but I have secured the two seats next to him."

I was directed to my seat and introduced to the Prince, who very graciously shook my hand, his other arm being immobilised by the largest Rolex I have ever seen. Throughout the whole performance I was enveloped in a lavender mist of

---

28 The ancient Christian community of Egypt.

almost tangible aftershave. The concert, all local talent, was excellent, and a further highlight was the compère, who, after each round of applause, would walk up to the front of the stage, his hands raised, and say in English, "Thank you, thank you for the clap."

The first time he said it, Ali spun round in his seat, his hand over his mouth, clearly on the verge of hysterics. He had been around British soldiers too long.

The last major event in the visit was a boat trip to the Temple of Philae. This was another UNESCO rescue project that had been re-sited. As we approached the small boat ramp where the taxis ply their trade, our attention was caught by a group of German high-school girls waiting to board. Their attention, in turn, was caught by the government limo and the smart salute of a local soldier. Ali was set to requisition the boat, but I gestured to him to let them all on. This he did, and then during the journey, they were wondering who I could possibly be. At one point he was actually asked by one of the girls, and he turned to me and whispered, "These lovely *fräuleins* want to know who you are. Who do you want to be?"

I thought about it, and told him, "Anyone, as long as it is not someone who is supposed to speak German."

He nodded, and turned to the girl who had posed the question, and looking around, said, "You have the honour of being in the presence of His Highness the Prince of Norway. But for security reasons, you must not reveal this, and *no* photos."

Her awe was evident, and so was mine. The rest of the day was spent in the company of these flaxen-haired acolytes, who nicely complemented the temples.

After an extraordinary week, and a brief elevation to the nobility, I had to leave for a more prosaic existence. Ali came with me, directing me to the VIP lounge, where I sat alone except for HE the Ambassador of a bankrupt French African nation and his wife, on their way to a shopping spree in Paris.

I wonder whether he realised he was in the company of HRH the Prince of Norway?

Ali's ruminations on the security situation, aboard the *felucca* in the light of early evening, proved to be only too tragically true. In October of the following year, 1990, Rifaat El-Mahgoub, Speaker of Parliament, my host, was assassinated. Al-Gama'a Al-Islamiyya militants, seeking to assassinate then Interior Minister Abdel-Halim Moussa, killed him by mistake.

14

Elephant, white nights and an amorous hound

Leningrad, 1990

DURING MY TIME as a visiting professor at Moscow State University in 1990, many interesting things occurred. Perhaps not the least of these was the total disappearance of the USSR as I slept. But the focus of this tale is in a time before that strange affair came to pass.

Central to everything that is about to happen is the larger-than-life figure of Dr Batoyan, Soviet Armenian professor of oceanography and *entrepreneur extraordinaire* who embodied every skill necessary to survive and advance in the erstwhile

USSR. He was a tall, swarthy individual with flashing eyes and the de rigueur Caucasian black moustache. Never seen without a leather jacket, he looked more like Central Casting's choice for a Mafia hit man than a distinguished oceanographer. Cousteau he was not. At one point he had spent time on some sort of 'fraternal mission' in Cuba, where he had picked up Spanish. Since he was more comfortable speaking that language than English, he would dart about interlinguistically without hesitation or warning. Almost every statement began with the word *entonces* (then), which I first took to be a reference to his tonsils until I realised that we had switched languages. Neither his mind nor his body was ever still. It seemed that there was almost nothing he could not do or improvise. I remember a time when he was showing me some experimental research equipment based on lasers. I paused for a moment before the complexity of it all, and then asked him, "Isn't that item in the middle a food mixer?"

"I have to finish this experiment before my wife starts baking," was his explanation.

As part of my visit, between classes, my colleagues worked hard to keep me amused. To assist in this endeavour Dr Batoyan suggested a trip to Leningrad – as it still was then, but not for long. I thought that going anywhere with Dr B would be what is now called 'a total experience'. I was not disappointed.

The original plan had been that there would be three of us, but whoever was supposed to be joining Dr Batoyan failed to materialise. As the time of departure drew nigh and it seemed certain the friend was not coming, Dr B rushed off into the crowd and approached a young woman whose face immediately brightened. It seems that he was not going to let the ticket go to waste, and the train was sold out, so he made a noble gesture and sold it to the lady for 50% of its face value. As always his entrepreneurial radar was on high intensity. Relieved of the ticket, and some roubles to the better, he rejoined me and said:

"*¡Vámonos!*"[29]

I had, in fact, made this journey once before, in 1963, and the train – and indeed the station – looked exactly the same, as though preserved in aspic since my last visit. The sturdy carriages were emblazoned with the coat of arms of the USSR and we were in first class – the explanation for which was, according to Dr Batoyan, "Otherwise we would be crushed by workers and peasants."

He had revealed his somewhat less than mainstream view of Marxist-Leninist orthodoxy the day before, when he had taken me to see a very fine, and very old, Orthodox Church. The weather was bad, and when we parked, he locked the car very securely, and then proceeded to take off both windscreen wipers. I had never seen anyone do this before, so I had to ask him why. His answer was, "If I don't take them off and carry them with me when I leave the car, then they will be subject to socialist redistribution."

"What's that?" I asked.

"They will be stolen," he explained.

Despite the fact that the train was 'full' there was no-one in the compartment we occupied. During the course of the journey, people would occasionally stop by and enquire hopefully whether there were any seats available, at which point he spoke to them in a very rapid and animated, if not slightly deranged, way. They left as though they had been told that the plague had been identified in this very spot. Quite possibly, given my later experiences, that was exactly what they *were* told. Before settling down in our splendid isolation, Dr Batoyan started to place his luggage up on the racks. This led me to ask him why he had three suitcases, including one very large one that was astonishingly heavy. We were, as I understood it, going for only three days, and all I had with me was a small backpack.

---

29 'Let's Go!'

"Well," he started, "there are three video machines in the big suitcase, the next suitcase is full of essential supplies for the journey, and the little case has all my stuff."

I wondered what sort of essential supplies we needed, because it looked as though he could have a mobile field hospital in that medium-sized case.

It seemed that we had urgent need of essential supplies forthwith, because he leapt up, and wrestled down the battered old middle case that he had just put on the rack above my head. Very gingerly he lowered it onto one of the vacant seats and proceeded to open it, which included the removal of a large encircling leather belt. As he slowly opened the lid, he looked at me with a knowing smile, and said, "Where would you like to start?"

Apart from alcohol of every sort – well, not *every* sort, because I saw only spirits – there was nothing else in the case. If we consumed all these 'essential supplies' on this trip, not only would we have no livers at the end of the three days, but also it is very unlikely that our bodies would decompose, being so thoroughly pickled.

"Do you seriously intend that we should get through that lot on this trip?" I enquired, astonished.

"Of course not, but we must be ready to entertain at any moment; I could be looking out of that window into the corridor, and some lovely lady, in a very dry condition, might be passing. It would not be polite to ignore such a thing," he observed, with one inquiring eyebrow raised.

I thought it best not to respond, especially as at that moment I was exactly three weeks away from my wedding. I made some sort of 'maybe later' gesture, and pointed to a bottle of *Ararat* Armenian cognac that turned out to be indescribably good – what I remember of it. This lubricated the conversation wonderfully, and I am not sure that I was not speaking Spanish within the hour.

He told me that Armenians were regarded as a sort of Mafia in Russia as they controlled a lot of the trade; both legal and illegal. I told him it was a reputation that was well served by his appearance. The Russians, he said, referred to everyone from the Caucasus (Armenians, Azeris, and Georgians) as 'Black' and considered them all to be suspicious, much like the way they viewed the gypsies. In fact, they produced a disproportionately large slice of the intellectuals, as well, of course, as Josef Stalin (Georgian) and the head of the KGB, Aliyev (Azeri). But, he went on, the Armenians did not have as bad a reputation as the folks from Azerbaijan, because they were not only Caucasians, but also *Turks* and Muslims. He leaned forward to tell me this, as though this was too awful to be spoken. Slowly, the pecking order of the USSR was beginning to emerge. But learning it in this broad-brush, thespian way was an entertainment as well as an educational process. The old adage 'The swiftness of the hand deceives the eye' was definitely true as far as that bottle of *Ararat* was concerned, and I thought for the longest time that I was slowly sipping the same drink. We were probably in double figures by that point.[30] It was beginning to become a little disorienting – the cognac, the curiously Victorian décor of the compartment, and tales of the Caucasus that could have come from Leo Tolstoy himself.

Just as sleep was making its claim on both of us, a gentleman entered wanting to make up the beds, and so we joined the other 80% of the passengers who were smoking in the corridor. We leaned out of the window staring into the night sky, relying on the window for support – at least I did, but I think I was out of my league here because Dr B was as alert and on the qui vive as ever.

Dawn came, revealing a landscape that looked exactly like the one we had left behind before sleeping. But I was assured that we were "almost there". I felt wonderful, despite the cognac diet. We disembarked with some difficulty, given the number

---

30 *Ararat* refers to Mount Ararat where Noah ended up parking the Ark. This is sacred to the Armenians, but is actually situated in Turkey, though clearly visible from Armenia's capital, Yerevan.

and weight of the suitcases, despite our best efforts to lighten the load the previous night. Quickly we were assisted by one of my companion's national network of friends and hustled away to our hotel. This edifice, the *Pribaltiyskaya* ('next to the Baltic') was new and very solid in a proletarian sort of way. It doubled as the terminal for the ferry service across the Gulf of Finland to, well, Finland. It was, therefore, a point of entry into the USSR and supported a large complement of KGB frontier police, sporting their distinctive green epaulettes – still a curious sight for someone from the West, though the KGB was far from the power it had been. (As Dr B put it, "Once they kept the crime down, now half the time they *are* the crime.")

We checked in at one of those Soviet attempts at modernism that somehow never seem to work. In this case it was partly a problem of juxtaposing some naturally beautiful material, usually marble, with trashy anodised-metal fittings, out-of-control chandeliers, and a zero-maintenance problem. Unusually vile was the lavish use of white tile that made everything look like a monstrously huge *pissoir*. I was about to say something, when Dr B introduced me to a couple of his friends that he had noticed in the atrium. It was only by the grace of God that I had kept my mouth shut, because the lady in the party turned out to be the architect responsible for the runaway porcelain. How is it possible to make a building look shoddy when it is new? That will remain one of the great secrets that the USSR took to its geopolitical grave.

Another peculiarity of Russian hotels was (and maybe is, but I doubt it) that externally they created an aura of hugeness and splendour, and then internally the basic services were improvised, amateur and capricious. Rooms were poky and corridors vast. Classically, in this case breakfast became a notoriously movable feast. Just because you had it here yesterday does not mean that you will get it here tomorrow – or anywhere, ever. In this instance, breakfast was picked up, infantry fashion, from a man behind a counter as and when he decided it was time to eat. A menu was unnecessary because all the options were there in front of you (and him). The first morning I enjoyed some rather delicious eggs, but they never appeared again, and after that breakfast was both a temporal and spatial mystery that we never solved.

Once I had unloaded my modest luggage, I went to find Dr B. He was in the foyer with the same couple, who were just leaving *with his big suitcase*. Aha. Right away, he snapped into action and said, "What would you like to do?", which suited me well because I cannot bear to hang around hotels once I have arrived somewhere. I want to see what is happening. I suggested we go out into the town and just walk around, especially after that extremely long train journey.

He tried and tried to hail a cab, often exchanging words with the driver, who would then drive off, leaving us helpless. Since we had no specific destination, I could not imagine what their problem could be. Eventually he said that the rouble was so weak, inflation so rapid, and the price of gasoline rising so fast that the taxi drivers would not take anyone unless they had US dollars. I had those in abundance, but it was extremely embarrassing for my host to ask me for money, and I felt very bad for him. On the other hand, we were going nowhere unless something changed. I proposed that I sell him the dollars (actually only $2). That saved face and by waving them vigorously he effectively stopped a lumbering old brown Volga that took us off to a picturesque part of the city.

Leningrad[31] was built on a swamp by means of driving hundreds of thousands of piles into the marshes to support the buildings. Peter the First intended it to be Russia's 'window on the west' and principal port. To deal with the problem of tides and drainage, the city is a maze of canals, earning it the name 'The Venice of the North' (along with Stockholm and a few other places). Peter had the city built at a very appropriate time architecturally, and he secured the services of many fine,

31 I will use the name Leningrad because that is what it was while I was there, and that is how I remember it.

mainly Italian, architects to design the monumental structures. It comes across as noble and architecturally harmonious, like Paris but unlike London, which is now a patchwork riparian mess. Even bearing in mind the Soviet absence of maintenance and the consequent careworn outward appearance of the buildings, Leningrad is still a marvellous and inspiring sight.

On this particular day, we were simply to stroll, though in the afternoon I was being handed off temporarily to a colleague of Dr B's who would work that shift. The day was perfect, and the surroundings ideal for a promenade. Before long we came across a wedding in full swing. The bride and groom were posing on the steps of a storybook intensely blue Orthodox church, with newly gilded onion domes shimmering and blazing in the noonday sun. Dr B noticed that I was taking a photograph of the group, and so without a word he went over to them and told them to face me, which they happily did, not knowing who on earth we were. In the past, Dr B observed, it was customary for the bride and groom to go off and be photographed near a statue of Lenin or, at one time, Stalin.

We meandered on, working up something of an appetite. Privatisation was still in its infancy at this time, and, to a westerner, the number of places to eat remained absurdly small for such a major city, though there was explosion of new eateries soon after. In fact, we could not find anywhere to eat, but one has to bear in mind that the summer of 1990 was a time of serious crisis in the USSR and food was completely absent from the market. For instance, many of the grocery shops in Moscow were totally empty. The only place we could find at all was a new-looking stall in the square that fronted St Isaac's Cathedral. The language that advertised the stallholder's wares was totally impenetrable. It seemed to consist of a random splattering of strings of vowels, with and without umlauts. The language turned out to be Finnish – Finland is, after all, just down the road from Leningrad. Some enterprising Finn had opened this facility selling all sorts of imported edible luxuries. The catch was that the prices were in Finnish markka, a currency I had neither seen nor heard of. This put Dr B back in the same dilemma as before; first as a host, and second as a Caucasian, whose hospitality is legendary. We agreed another international loan, this day beginning to feel like taking a vacation with the IMF. But with the financial crisis resolved, the food hit the spot, and we were reinvigorated. Dr B constantly enquired whether I would like to see this or that museum, but to be honest I was enjoying myself far too much wandering around in his wonderfully unpredictable company to want to hide away inside a museum.

At one point, we were sprawled on a bench watching life go by and discussing the black market (Dr B was appropriately done out this day in a brown leather jacket, prominent sunglasses and a perpetual cigarette), when he suddenly said, "Let's go and see the *Aurora*."

So we walked over to where the venerable battleship was moored. Well, a glance into the water revealed that she was more than moored; she was seemingly fixed in place forever. Nevertheless, the ship was a remarkable piece of solid historical ironmongery, still looking more or less as she must have appeared in 1917 when the sailors fired a shot at the Winter Palace, not to dislodge the Tsar, for he was long gone, but to speed up the departure of Kerensky's Democratic Government.

It must have helped, since Kerensky, a man of strange emotions, given to bursting into tears at cabinet meetings, was overthrown and went into exile after a brief and frenzied period as leader of Russia. It was hard to imagine that someone who led Russia in 1917–18 would be living in California in the 1960s and lecturing at Stanford until he died in 1970. It was equally strange to look at this superannuated naval relic and realise that it had actually fired rounds, albeit blank, at a Stanford professor who was teaching when I was.

Dr B, as always, was full of even more surprises. He told me that the *Aurora* had been at the disastrous naval battle of Tsushima in 1905, when the Japanese destroyed the 'entire Russian fleet'. Well, clearly some of the fleet survived. He further explained that the *Aurora* had not fired the first shot in the Revolution – the shot for which she is remembered was, in fact, a blank shell signalling the attack on the Winter Palace. Mr Kerensky, meanwhile, had wisely escaped in a cab, apparently disguised as a woman. Furthermore, Dr B continued, the ship went on to see active duty in World War II before being laid to rest as a tourist attraction. For many people in 1990, the *Aurora* was still something of a shibboleth because of her iconic role in the events of the Revolution. When I visited her, she was more of a naval curiosity, offering tourists dinner on board.[32]

At this point, Dr Batoyan had to head off to Leningrad University, so he handed me over to his friend Sergei, who was stocky, handsome and topped off with a shock of red hair, which usually denotes someone from Odessa.[33] His English was easy and comfortable, and he promised to be a good guide and companion. He suggested a short saunter to see some of the sights, but in fact we ended up standing on one of the bridges over the Neva in a sort of reverie gazing at the elegant pastel-coloured edifices and the eternal fascination of river traffic.

In this comfortable and relaxing environment, Sergei began talking about his past, still something of a novelty with a foreigner in the fast-changing USSR. His early career had been in the Soviet Navy, where he had risen to be the commander of a submarine (shades of Tom Clancy?), but he was clearly not in the navy now, so I asked him why he had changed.

"I was always trying to practise my English, though we were not supposed to have contact with people from the West, especially military people. But one night in a bar, I got into a fight with some American sailors, and eventually the police arrived, so the news got out and I was dismissed. It was really stupid." Since then he had been studying English and had gone back to school. That was the story.

---

32 She was later overhauled and recommissoned as flagship of the Russian Navy in 2016.

33 Danny Kaye was a good example of just such a person.

He checked his watch and told me that our destination was the Hermitage Museum, which is really a collection of museums like the Smithsonian. It includes the Winter Palace. The term 'Hermitage' originally referred to a small theatre with almost perfect acoustics that is still in use. The name is usually applied now to the main art collection, especially the extraordinary display of leading Impressionists. There is a tendency to think of Russia historically as a sprawling heterogeneous continental empire under an iron regime of oriental despotism that did not share in the transforming European experiences such as the Enlightenment, the Renaissance, and the Industrial Revolution, and which was separated from the West by Russia's own Orthodox form of Christianity. That may all be true in a strict sense of shared experience, but Peter the Great certainly did not fit that mould. Certainly he was an unrestrained autocrat, but also a moderniser and innovator, with an especial reverence for the Dutch. In fact he spent time among them masquerading as a shipbuilder and learning the trade. He drew in legions of Germans and other Europeans to move his country forward, and especially to create his new capital city. Indeed, some of his leading military commanders were Scotsmen. Continuing this tradition of acquiring the best from the West, Catherine the Great, certainly no democrat herself, instructed her ministers abroad to scour Europe for the finest examples of art – established and innovative. Thus she amassed an enormous collection of the best representative paintings of the period. This tradition continued, along with Italian architecture, German porcelain, and the use of French at Court. In this way, Russia came to have an astounding heritage of Rembrandts, French Impressionists, and even a Da Vinci.

When we entered the building via a superabundance of marble and malachite, we found a long line of people waiting to buy tickets. I moved to join them, but Sergei directed me to follow him to front of the queue. I assumed he had already purchased tickets. Instead he flashed a small red booklet at the guard, and we went through. I was impressed, so said to him,

"I see you come here often, since you have a pass to enter."

With a smile, he reached into his pocket, extracted the card and showed it to me. Stamped in gold on the front were the three Cyrillic letters 'KGB'.

"That," he observed, "is a pass to anywhere. Very useful." Another man of mystery and surprises.

The paintings were overwhelming, but the display rather unimaginative and extremely crowded. On the other hand, it was possible to get intimately close to these masterpieces. We came to the Van Gogh collection in its own empty, undistinguished room, and I lingered rather longer there. In front of one particularly bold piece, I remarked to Sergei, "This is such a beautiful painting, but, you know, you can't really appreciate his unique skill with colour because of the way the painting is placed. You see, if you stand in front of it, the light from one of the windows is right in your line of vision."

"Absolutely so," he commented, standing beside me and moving his head around. Then, to my horror, he reached up and *took the painting off the wall* and held it in front of him. "Is this better?" he asked, moving around slightly to find the best light, while I prepared for all hell to break loose. Nothing happened. Then he insisted that I hold it, and he took a picture of me with it. At that, he put it back, all $50 million of it, and we went on. That was a solidly proletarian view of art, I thought, sharing it with the masses. I thanked Sergei for a unique experience, and we proceeded through the Malachite Hall to the exit, where Dr B was waiting.

"Was it fun?" he enquired, his arm around Sergei's shoulder.

"More than I could have imagined," I said. "The KGB and Van Gogh in the same day are definitely fun. What now?"

"Now we go to the Smolny[34] to meet my old friend, who will give us lunch."

---

34 The Institute, formerly a rather exclusive school for young ladies, became headquarters during the Revolution when the Bolsheviks seized power from Mr Kerensky's Provisional Government.

This we did, and in front of the blue and white Smolny Institute was his friend – *all* of him. He was *enormous*, smiling and clearly pleased to see us. I shook his vast hand, and Dr B said, "This is my friend, and we all call him Elephant, for reasons I do not need to explain. He will take us to his apartment, which is very nice because he is an architect."

Replacing his windscreen wipers, Elephant ushered us into his new Lada, and we went to his home. It was, like all Russian apartments, small, but very well appointed and suffused with an excellent ambience of creativity. His wife Irina[35] was there to greet us, just as warmly as her husband had. As is normal in Russia, the table was set, the food was out, and everything was ready to go – there are no preliminaries to a meal. We sat down, and started on the cold *hors d'ouvres*, which were splendid, especially given the aforementioned lack of food in the shops at this point in Russian history.

"How do you find all this food?" I asked, rather ungraciously.

To which Elephant replied, through Dr B, "The food, like everything else, is always there; you just need to know where *there* is. In the past, for example, you would go into the furniture stores, and they would show you a catalogue – there was never anything good in the store. You would select your choice, and they would say, 'Oh, sorry, that one is completely sold out, but I think I could find one for you, but it will cost you double.' Now, of course, what was happening was that the people in the store were buying all the best items themselves and then selling them to us at three times the price. I think it is called capitalism." He laughed, and continued, "And Dr Batoyan here is the master of market economics." My mind went back to the big suitcase.

Gesturing across the table, Irina told us to start, and Dr B unloaded a couple of bottles from his plastic bag, probably from the medium-sized suitcase. The toasts began at once,

---

35 Because of what follows, I cannot swear to the authenticity of the name.

initially to the host, the cook, the university, and all sorts of reasonable things. It rapidly degenerated into an excuse for more spirits dedicated to ever more trivial causes. Both vodka and cognac circulated freely. The food relentlessly continued to appear, and at one moment, Dr B asked me, "Now, you see old Elephant there – where do you think he had his last job?"

I had not a shred of guidance on where an oversized Russian architect would have worked previously. Irina chipped in to say that we were using the wrong term, as he was not an architect, he was a graphic designer. Ah. But that did not help me at all. I gave up, having nothing to build my inquiry upon.

"Antarctica!" said Dr B with a flourish. "He was with our base down there, well protected from the cold by all that fat!"

I never actually discovered what a graphic designer was doing down there, but we toasted penguins and snow and who knows what. So it continued until, replete, we retired for coffee and chocolate to the bedroom.[36] There, over coffee, Irina – who was an artist – introduced me to the works of a Russian painter who was totally unknown to me: Ivan Bilibin. His paintings were breathtakingly bold and strong and had a hint of Art Nouveau blended with the sort of strong colour and firm line that I associated with book illustrations for children in the 1930s. Irina gave me a beautiful book on his life, mercifully in English.

The coffee having long since expired, the men remorselessly refilled my shot glass as the conversation continued. It ended – at least for me – when I passed out backwards. Luck was with me, because I was sitting on the end of the bed.

When I woke up, I was aware of two things. First, the sun was still shining brightly, and second, someone else was also recumbent on the bed and rather intimately tucked in close behind me. In response to the former, I was happy that I had not been out too long, and to the latter, I did not know what to

---

36 Russian apartments are so small that rooms often have more than one purpose, and are set out accordingly.

think. Apart from the body heat, I could hear heavy breathing and then someone was gently licking my neck. And here was I, about to be married.

I steeled myself to resolve this remarkable situation, and turned over to find myself staring into the deep brown eyes of a huge Great Dane. He licked my nose. It came as quite a shock – first that it was a dog, and second, that it was the size of the average horse – but was unlikely to compromise my nuptials. Eventually my host ventured in, relieved me of the dog and said we would all benefit from a long walk. The weather was good and it seemed like an excellent idea.

The streets were busy, and we walked around without any real purpose for quite some time. After a while, Dr B said that we should go to the river and see what was happening, and maybe go to the beach near the St Peter and Paul Fortress. So we waited at a bus stop for quite a while, until a bus eventually stopped – with some encouragement from Dr B, who stood in its path. The driver told him that the bus was finished for the day, and was going back to the terminus. I looked at my watch, and this seemed a little unlikely for 3 p.m. Dr Batoyan, with his irresistible charm and even more irresistible bankroll, convinced the driver to turn the bus around completely, and take us to the beach. This he did. After our arrival, we had a brief encounter with a rock concert – again something new, but much too frenzied for us. In the end we moved away, sat on the beach and discussed all sorts of things.

Eventually, I said, "This has been a busy day, I can't believe it's only four o'clock. I suppose we should head for the hotel for dinner?"

"Dinner?" asked Mr Batoyan. "You mean breakfast. It is four in the morning. You must be confused by the fact that these are the White Nights."

"*White Nights?*"

"Yes, this far north, in June, the sun never really sets and so it is light in the night."

No wonder I felt disoriented; I had slept a lot longer than I thought! But Dr B agreed we should return as Elephant had to work the following day – no, in four hours. Dr B then started closely monitoring the traffic on the river, and suddenly jumped to his feet and from the water's edge started waving his arms at one boat. As it pulled toward us, I realised it was a police river-patrol vessel. Dr B worked his charm on them, and in the company of the law we made our way toward the dawn and the ferry terminal that was one side of our hotel.

The final day, a Sunday, was reserved for a visit to the Kunstkammer. This is one of the world's more interesting museums because it panders to the human fascination with the grotesque. Peter the Great, Russia's Renaissance Man, spent quite some time in the Netherlands, as we noted earlier. While there, he came into contact with Frederik Ruysch, who was a faculty member of the University of Leiden's distinguished Anatomy School. Among his many talents, Dr Ruysch was a truly remarkable embalmer and his subjects remained uncannily lifelike. Twice weekly he opened his 'cabinet' to the general public, who were able to view a collection of embalmed children in various attitudes of repose in small coffins. For this, in the best Dutch tradition, he charged a fee.

One day in 1697, the enormous and intimidating figure of the Tsar paid a visit. He was instantly captivated by the whole display, even to the extent of kissing one of the children. He came back for several return visits, never losing his excitement, until eventually he offered to buy the entire collection. It took him twenty years, and the unheard of figure of 30,000 guldens, until he eventually got the lot in 1728. Ten years earlier, inspired by his visit to Dr Ruysch, he had issued a decree requiring the people of Russia to bring forth all their 'monsters' and he amassed a considerable collection – both living and dead. The Kunstkammer was built, in part, to house these specimens. And, to this day, there they reside for all to see.

But not us, because the notice on the door said they closed on Sundays. This was a huge disappointment, because I had heard so much about this place. For me, that would have been the end of the affair – but not for my resourceful companion.

"In Russian we have a saying: 'Every house has two doors, one in the front and the other in the back'," he said.

With that, he turned and walked briskly to, not exactly the back door, but a tiny door in the side that was not entirely closed.

Inside the dark room, we could barely make out the form of a *babushka* asleep on a couch (maybe she was part of the collection?). Dr B's entry woke her in a state of alarm and confusion, which worked very much to his advantage. In rapid Russian, he bombarded the woman with some story, too fast for me, but I did pick up on the expression "President of Yale University". The *babushka* leapt to her feet and telephoned someone. The word "Director" appeared several times in the conversation, as did that enigmatic President of Yale. The old lady informed us that the Director would be here very shortly. It seems that the back door had opened.

As a matter of fact, a very charming lady arrived very quickly, and personally escorted us around the entire collection. The Kunstkammer is no less interesting for being a museum itself, conveying how people in the early eighteenth century thought a display should be organised. It was made more intimate by the wide use of wood, and the fact that all the display cabinets, etc., were made by hand. Also, there was clearly much less concern in those days about the malevolent instincts of the visiting public, as things were far more 'up close and personal'. It was Peter the Great's ambition to modernise Russia, and make the country and its people more aware of science. There is, of course, an element of the 'freak show' about having so many preserved human specimens on show, but that was not his intention. On the other hand, people were less reserved about their fascination with deformity in those times, indeed Mr Barnum staked his money on it much later. The fascination is still there, but it is not polite to express it now, unless you subscribe to the *National Enquirer*.

Undeniably, Dr Ruysch did have a remarkable skill, because many of his 'specimens', deformities aside, were so evidently alive at one time, that 'specimen' seemed hardly an appropriate word to use. It is also remarkable to see such perfectly preserved specimens of people, some of whom died before America gained its independence. Normally they would have lived out their lives, returned to dust, and been totally forgotten. Now they are eternal, for though their earthly lives were extremely short in most cases, they remain always with us, locked in a state of everlasting infancy. Instead of the uncomfortable feeling I get watching a Fellini movie, with its predictable passing parade of grotesques, this was very moving and a stark reminder of mortality. It was also salutary to look at the selfsame specimens that had so moved Peter the Great and inspired him to acquire the collection for Russia.

On that rather sombre note, our visit to Leningrad came to an end, and we made our way back to the train station. The return journey to Moscow was enlivened by Dr B's foray into the corridor to invite a very comely blonde Russian lady to join us. She did, and he proceeded to tell her how I could think of nothing but her surpassing beauty since I had first glimpsed her in the corridor. She was pleased to hear this, though it was the first that I knew of it, and on my unwilling behalf, he provided her with my address at Moscow State. Mercifully nothing ensued from that well-meaning matchmaking effort.

When we arrived in much more mundane Moscow, Dr B scanned the platform in all directions for his student, whose task it was to collect us. Eventually the man arrived and Dr B said, "Help carry these bags to the car."

"There is no car," the student apologised.

"How come?"

"Well, the car is fine, but when I went down to start it this morning, all the wheels were gone."

"Socialist redistribution has reached wheels," Dr Batoyan exclaimed, probably wondering whether he would now have to take the wheels with him every time he left his car.

15

The unexpected stripper

Orlando, Florida, 1993

Our location: Orlando Florida; the time: the early 1990s. Though it is a little-known fact, there *are* people who go to Orlando without ever visiting, or intending to visit, Disney's Magic Kingdom. Nevertheless, the place can hold some magical moments even outside the enchanted borders of the Rodent's realm.

Conferences – and that is why I was there – have only two functions: shopping and networking. The rest is all space-filling, tedious beyond words and pretentious beyond measure. People strive to climb the conference hierarchy just as viciously as they scale the corporate ramparts. I can think of no worse cause to which to sacrifice an otherwise fulfilling and fun-filled life. At the time this story takes place, my principal concern was not with pushing back the frontiers of knowledge, but checking out the shopping mall. I had been told that there was an "interesting mall" somewhat out of town, but it was worth the ride. I took them at their word and hailed a cab, the driver of which was quite happy to drive me there.

When we arrived, it was late afternoon and I arranged with the driver that he would come back and pick me up at the same place two hours from then. He happily agreed and drove off. The mall certainly was stupendous, and brilliantly illuminated by virtue of its vast glass roof. Otherwise, it had been pretty well homogenised into the generic species *Mallus mallus*, so if you were parachuted in blindfolded, you would not know if you were in San Diego or Asbury Park, or anywhere else for that matter. I began to wonder after the first half-hour how I was going to fill the rest of the time. Next to the entrance where I was to meet the taxi, there was a store devoted solely to Hallowe'en (this being September). The American year has been subtly remodelled into New Year, Easter, Mother's Day, St Patrick's Day, Boss's Day (16 October), Kwanzaa (26 December to 1 January), and many, many more Hallmarked occasions. By this time, I noticed that the mall was being plunged into ever-greater darkness. People gathered around the door looking at the most intensely black sky I have ever seen, and more interesting still – it was closing on us fast. The blackness was occasionally thrown into sharp counterpoint by wild lightning flashes that I thought, up to this point, occurred only in cartoons or Greek myths. This approaching weather system was almost visibly swallowing up the daylight in the way that Stephen King's Langoliers gobbled up the past. The inky clouds were connected to the earth by an almost solid wall of water that it dragged over the sodden surface of the land.

Within the mall, not much had changed, because the lighting came on and turned us into a lonely island of radiance facing down the tsunami of cloud and rain preparing to break over us. Still, insulated as most of us are from any true contact with Nature, the whole thing was really on the scale of a rather oversized IMAX performance.

It was then that the lights went out. The Langoliers had gobbled us up in one bite, and I was standing in the Hallowe'en Shop in total darkness. Somewhere some feeble emergency lighting kicked in, turning the inky blackness into a much-more intimidating faint silhouette of Draculoid shapes. Then a truly Zeusian thunderbolt struck this false god of modern commerce with elemental fury. The building shook, and for one brief moment of harsh blue light, I was transported straight into *Friday the 13th*. That almost ended the story right there. I groped my way out of this chamber of horrors, and lightning flash by lightning flash I made my way to the main exit. We had all been suddenly sent into 'Strobe World', where people existed in flashes like a very bad, very early attempt at moving pictures.

Flash! The lights came back and our response was to freeze until we realised that normality, of a sort, had returned. On the other hand, outside the glass doors there was a living reenactment of the *Poseidon Adventure*; the rain really appeared to have coalesced into something like the back end of Niagara Falls. People waited until their lifts pulled up at the entrance and then ran helter-skelter for the open car door. Umbrellas were out of the question, because the time necessary to close the umbrella in order to get into the car would result in a near-drowning experience.

There was not the slightest indication that the cloudburst was anywhere near drawing to a close. The sky overhead remained an intense black.

Then, just like waiting on Death Row, or preparing to make that first parachute jump, my moment came. There before me, pulling into the kerb was the Yellow Cab with my driver waving furiously at me. He threw open the rear door, I put down my head and decided the best way to do this was to dive right across the back seat and he could close the door by pulling away sharply. With a "Geronimo!" to the waiting crowd around the door, I hurtled through the rain that was already through my coat and working its way through my shirt. Judging the distance as best I could, I poised myself and took off in my best Indiana-Jones-into-the-abyss dive. I made it perfectly.

The scream was totally unexpected. I wondered what I had done to myself to elicit such a shriek. The cab lurched off, the door slammed shut, and I was trying to work out why my legs were horizontally across my face. But wait, I definitely had not beenwearing tights when I got in. In one hand I was clutching the hem of a really flimsy mini skirt, and you do not want to know where the other one was. I quickly shot up into a vertical position, and found myself sitting next to a scantily dressed, highly made-up young woman in a state of shock. We shared at least that. The driver, a Lebanese fellow, turned around and said:

"I'm sorry, boss, but she jumped in as I was waiting at the stop sign on the corner before I got to you. I mean, in this weather, I could hardly throw her out. But this *is* your cab, and so you must decide before I proceed. Whatjathink?"

She fixed me with a look of supplication encircled by some of the longest artificial eyelashes I had yet encountered. She fluttered them encouragingly.

"No, there is no way we can hurl this lady into the night, plus this road is fast becoming a river." Turning to the victim of the rugby tackle, I asked: "Where exactly do you need to go?"

Her destination was on the Strip (use your imagination), and the taxi driver chipped in with, "Hey, Boss, that's the whole other end of the town from your hotel. It's going to add quite a bit to the fare and the time – so youse going to have to resolve that."

He was addressing me via the rear-view mirror. How could I be anything but a gallant host in circumstances as meteorologically inclement as this?

"Let's go," I said heartily.

The driver's eyes (all I could see of him) flickered between deep respect and total disbelief, but off we went. The young lady turned to me and said, "What a guy. I really, really want to thank you. What's your name?"

I told her but she heard it as Rudolph, so I spent the rest of the journey under this festively Christmas-oriented moniker. I thought that might have been that. But no. She sat back, and then said to the car in general, "Can you believe this? I met this guy in the Mall while I was doing some shopping, like for intimate things, you know. He was a cool guy, and I think we sort of, like, fell in love, you know..."

I interrupted briefly, "Are we talking about *this afternoon?*"

"Sure, right, yes, this afternoon at the sandwich bar. He asked me what I was doing, and I told him I was looking for some different underwear – I'm like, in show business and what I show is mostly my underwear." Her destination made some sense now. She continued, "So I brought out my bag and began to show him what I had bought. Hey, do you want to see?"

This was, most definitely, a rhetorical question because she was already up to her shoulders in the plastic bag sorting through a considerable quantity of lingerie of some sort. Then she whipped out a black lace thong that must have weighed less than a hummingbird:

"This is cute, but I couldn't find the matching top, so I will have to use it later in the show."

The parade of underwear continued, and there were a couple of items with tassels and some whose purpose I never could divine. After a representative sample, she put her purchases on the seat between us.

By now, the driver was entering the Strip, but right then it looked like Florida's answer to Venice. The driver eased the cab forward slowly along what he thought to be the road. The water level rose rapidly up the side of the car. There was another car, of course, right on our tail, which prevented us from reversing out of the dilemma. The driver threw his hands in the air and said, "Hell, I don't even know if I am on a road here, guys. I will take it slowly, if you don't mind."

We inched forward, and I had the distinct impression that we had moved from a terrestrial to an aquatic mode of transportation. The water coming in through the bottom of the door and flooding my shoes quickly drove this belief home. My partner had already lifted her knees to her chin. Mercifully, we rejoined terra firma almost immediately, though everything around us was under water. However, the car in front of us stalled, and we were, for the moment, stuck.

"Hey, guys," she interjected. "The reason I was in the cab was because this guy, this miserable bastard, dumped me in the Mall. I am asking you as men – can you believe that? I was abandoned, left to get home on my own, and he didn't even leave me the fare [oh, oh]. Can you believe that he just dumped me in such a situation?'

"Especially as you had grown so close," I added for emphasis.

"Yeah, that's right. One minute he is all over me and the next minute he storms out of there, leaving me without even paying for the drink. I am disgusted."

Ever in search of the truth of cause and effect, I asked her, while draining the water out of my shoes, "Did he give you any reason? I mean you are a very charming and personable young woman. I cannot imagine just walking out on you."

She looked at me in encouraging agreement, nodding vigorously and threw in, "You got it. After that phone call he was all fired-up to go."

"Phone call?" the taxi-driver and I said simultaneously.

"Right. He heard his name coming out of the PA system, and so he dragged himself over to the phone. So he comes back looking like, all dramatic and things, and tells me his brother had been in a car crash and was paralysed in the hospital and his mother wanted him at the hospital pronto because of some operation. Now, you know, that's kind of bad news, but to take off and dump me without even the taxi fare – that's cheap."

The driver and I both interjected vigorously with waving arms to break the flow, "Wait, wait – did you say his brother was paralysed in a car smash?"

"Yeah, sure, but it's not like he's going to die in the next ten minutes for God's sakes. Like this guy is hurtling out of the

Mall, and I am running like a maniac after him. He turned and said 'I gotta go, baby. Tough break.' *Tough break, my ass.* He was on this Harley – big spare seat and all – and I shouted, 'Can't you even drop me off?' He roared off, and I was pissed off. Damn – just dumping me like that."

Neither member of her audience quite knew how to handle this, but the driver caught my glance and told her, "Anyways. This nice gentleman has offered you this ride home, so things ain't so bad as it turns out."

"You are right," she replied, smiling at me. "But can you believe that that bastard dumped me?"

"Very bad form," I offered, though my prayers were with the Hog rider's brother.

Our companion vigorously waving her arms and shrieking avoided further discourse on this show of bad manners: "Here! Here! This is my motel, guys."

We were, in many ways, sad to part with our extraordinary new acquaintance. She bounced out of the car, leaned back in and said, "Hey, Rudolph, you was such a nice guy, would you like to come up and I can model some of this new fancy underwear for you. Some really great stuff, man."

The taxi driver's eyes were like over easy in the mirror. But I think I had reached my limit, so as graciously as I could, I declined the very generous offer.

"Rosie, I have to say it has been a unique experience meeting you, sharing your underwear and floating along the Strip in a Yellow Cab. I shall always remember it. You go lie down, relax and get this man out of your system. He was not for you."

Rosie looked, for just a moment, tearful, but quickly wiped that off with her shield of a smile: "Riighht. That's very, very true. OK, you guys. Off you go and don't get into trouble. Nice meeting you."

And she skipped up the stairs to the third floor, which was probably well above flood level.

The two pairs of eyes left in the car locked. He raised his eyebrows and rolled his eyes.

"What a character," I offered, to break the silence.

"Character? You ain't seen anything. She scores about a three. Now if she was high, drunk and violent, well, maybe a seven."

I was a bit intimidated by this, and told the driver that I would try to stick to three and below in future. I smiled at the memory of this unbelievable and unexpected journey and shook my head, and slapped my knees. I froze for a moment, and then slowly lifted a pink lacy thong embroidered with bluebirds into the view of the driver's mirror.

"Sweet," he said. "But be careful where you wear it."

"Home, James."

16

The elixir of life, eternal love, and a Swiss roll

On the shores of the Caspian Sea, 2000

WE WERE ON the Corniche: the broad seafront esplanade where the City of Baku – capital of Azerbaijan – meets the sea. The Caspian Sea, that is. Each evening the broad promenade is a gathering point for the residents of Baku, and it often looks as though everyone who lives in Baku is there. But this particular evening – my last – it was late, getting on for midnight, and as is customary on each of my last nights in the Paris of the Caucasus, I was with my good friend, bon vivant, and former student, Chingiz. Like many Azeris, he combines exquisite manners, old-fashioned charm and a wry sense of humour. He plunges into conversation, sounding out the deepest meanings of all aspects of life, going from zero to sixty in five seconds. From time to time, he is liable to drop some bombshell into the conversation, such as: "Tell me *honestly*, Dr Baker, do you really think Elvis might be alive?" This comes close on the heels of a discussion of the role of non-governmental organisations in a transitionary society. This is what makes conversation with him such a joy.

We had walked just about the length of the promenade, past the strange parabolic restaurant building left over from Soviet times, almost to where the docks begin. The waves lapped right up against the wall we were strolling by, and the lights of the city stretched all around us in a giant horseshoe. There were lights offshore too, because of the oil-drilling platforms, and indeed one entire city, five miles long, stood out there somewhere. Actually, we were strolling atop what was once the richest oilfield in the world, where the Nobel brothers came to make their fortunes, as did many Azeris in the days of the Russian Empire. Thanks to them, the promenade is backed by enormous houses incorporating curious mixtures of French Second Empire and Austrian Biedemeier, as well as the occasional flight of fancy running to turrets, gothic windows and whatever else took the eye of the late nineteenth century *nouveau riche*.

Over all of this, as a faintly discernable black, sombre presence, is the Maiden Tower – the symbol of the city. The tower is not actually attached to anything and has a curious shape, which, if seen from above, would resemble a comma. There are many, many stories about the origins of this unusual structure, which was at sea level when the Caspian was higher. The most popular story concerns a princess who was facing a wedding being forced upon her by an overbearing father, who was also, of course, the King. She despised her intended groom, and resisted all attempts to be married off to him. However, she knew that eventually she would be forced to wed for the sake of dynastic convenience. So she told her father, "I will agree to this marriage if you will agree to build me a tower from the top of which I may see the beauty of the Caspian Sea."

The father agreed, and a large structure was built. When finished, he showed it to her, but her response was not exactly what he had expected. "Father, it is a very fine tower, but not nearly high enough to do justice to the view."

So the king set out to add another level (we have no idea what the intended groom was doing during all this construction) until eventually this tower reached the limits of contemporary technology. The king explained, "We can give you no better view because we can go no higher without the structure crumbling under its own weight. How is the view now?"

The maiden wandered around the flat top of the tower, checking out the view in all directions. Then, judging the height to be adequate, she threw herself off the top. This left the king down one daughter, and in possession of a totally useless structure. Anyway, it has worn well, and is a very distinctive landmark. There is even a ballet about it.

By this time, Chingiz and I were not deconstructing the Maiden Tower conundrum so much as chatting over a midnight coffee at a table on the promenade. Time was not important, for my flight home did not leave until 4 a.m. and it was simply inconvenient to sleep for the short time that that departure allowed me.

We slowly became aware of a gentleman who was standing silently at the end of our table holding a small bottle. Chingiz engaged him in spirited conversation, and then turning to me, said, "We have here a gentleman here who has the elixir of life, no less. It is the residue of the repeated boiling of many thousands of some plant I never heard of. Anyway, his grandmother makes it and it takes months, years, I don't know, to produce a tiny amount. Are you interested?"

Most people are curious about something that prolongs life on earth. Heaven knows they have been searching long enough for the answer through many a fable and fairy tale. I thought legend had it that the elixir flowed out of a fountain. The contents of what Chingiz was holding would barely come out of the bottle. The distillate, sublimate, or whatever it was, had a very viscous nature and was of a dark brown colour.

The vendor motioned us to try it.

"Well, Chingiz, please tell him that I am more than ready to try it; but how do we find out if it works, other than sitting here for the next sixty years? It seems to me there is no way to run quality control on this substance. Ask him how he deals with that."

Chingiz, who loves these mind games, launched into a spirited exchange with the fellow. My friend has a very animated face, supplemented by gold-rimmed glasses and a moustache, as well as a huge and totally disarming smile. He is also very bold in his conversational style and body language. These tendencies have plunged him into deep water several times because he generally tends to say exactly what he thinks and 'damn the torpedoes'.

"Well now, he says that this miraculous substance is made only by his grandmother, and she is, as we speak, 112 years old. What is more, she lives in Nakhchivan, where many of the wise and powerful originate."[37]

"I see, so she is a sort of poster girl for the mixture?"

The gentleman's claim is not quite as absurd as you may at first think. The Caucasus is famous for extraordinarily long-lived people. On Mount Elbrus, in the Russian North Caucasus, I had come across a guide who was still taking people up the highest peak in Europe well after his hundredth birthday. And, just that week before Chingiz and I came together, I had visited the remote village of Lahej.

---

37 Nakhchivan is a curiosity because it is part of Azerbaijan, but since the Nagorno-Karabakh war with Armenia in the early nineties, it is totally cut off from the rest of Azerbaijan. Furthermore, it alone has a border – albeit a tiny one – with Turkey, Azerbaijan's natural ally. But, it is true that many prominent people have come from there, including the President at that time, Heydar Aliyev.

There I met a wonderful family who were friends of a friend and entertained me to lunch. On the wall of the house was a photograph – fairly recent – of a sturdy and spirited woman looking as though in her eighties. One of the gentlemen informed me that she had died that very year, and he was sad that I could not have met her because she was a wonderful person. I enquired how old she was when she died: one hundred and thirty two, he said, without emphasis. That meant she was born around the time the American Civil War broke out. The normal response to a statement like this is to assume it is probably not true and cannot be documented. But he produced papers, and even more logically, traced back marriages and births that showed she had to be that age.

On another occasion, I was shown a photograph of a couple celebrating their 100th wedding anniversary. That does not happen very often.

Bearing all this in mind, I said, "Tell him we'll take some," pointing at the bottle.

The man handed it over, and I looked forward to a long and bright future. On the other hand, bearing in mind my wedding was in 1998, when I was already over fifty, even the benefits of this liquid were unlikely to last until my 100th anniversary.

We move forward now two years. Once more, Chingiz was looking after me on my last, sleepless night in Baku. It was earlier in the day this time: twilight, to be exact. He and I were strolling along Istiglaliyyat Street, an imposing road that passes the Mayor's office and curves down toward the sea. We were heading for my hotel, which as before, was in the wonderfully preserved Old City, still encompassed by its massive walls and gates. To get into the Old City, we had to cross the street and pass the Metro and the bus station to reach the gate. Just as we approached the gate, it started to rain.

"There's a café right here in the bus terminus. Let's go and have a coffee until the rain stops," I suggested. I knew of it because someone had taken me there the previous evening when the weather had been much better.

"I have lived here all my life, and never encountered it," he said as we ran through the worsening rainstorm.

Once we were inside, a waiter suggested we go upstairs to the roof, where there was what the Viennese used to call a *chambre séparée*, though the purpose of the one in this restaurant was less daring than what the Austrians once used them for. We reached the room, shook off the rain, and sat at a simple table.

"Excuse me, Dr Baker: what refreshment would you like?"

"Tea will be fine for me."

At that point, the waitress entered. She was, like the other waitresses in this establishment, kitted out in what looked like an English schoolgirl's uniform: white shirt, pleated skirt (though they never came that short when I was in school), white ankle socks, and a striped tie that she had loosely knotted in front of the second or third button down on the shirt. This is curious enough in Baku, but the wearer looked just about the right age to be dressed this way. She had dark, closely-cropped hair, the largest and brightest eyes I have ever seen on anyone, and a smile to die for. She was the total ingénue.

Chingiz enquired whether she could provide a menu, and she gave a sad shake of the head, ending in a wicked smile.

"I see." Chingiz considered this. "Well, tell me what you have to drink and we will decide."

I think I had already decided, but the waitress went on to list everything she could think of, vigorously checking off each one on a different finger. Chingiz was clearly slightly out of his element here. As a married man with teenage children, he does not really live the life of the *boulevardier* that would bring him into these situations.

"Tea is fine for me," I repeated.

"Me too," he decided, and ordered two teas.

"Wait," I interjected, hoping to catch the waitress before she left. "Chingiz, we are likely to be here for some time – why don't we get a pot of tea?"

I sensed some disorder had entered the smooth flow of events, but Chingiz boldly repeated the request. The waitress raised her eyebrows and looked straight at me as though I was wearing two heads. She told Chingiz that she would see what she could do.[38] We lapsed into conversation, and soon the elfin schoolgirl was back with a tray. With great ceremony she lifted the pot high, sporting it to each side to show that she had accomplished her mission, and then put out a china sugar bowl and milk jug. She stood for a moment, looked contemplatively at the arrangement, then rearranged them, and smiled. After that she left, Oriental-style, walking backwards.

When Chingiz and I fell into an animated discussion, she came back. Chingiz, in mid-sentence, suddenly became aware of her presence and in surprise asked, "Yes, what do you want?"

"Is everything OK?" she asked him.

To me, having lived in America, this is perfectly natural. In Baku it is more than unusual.

"OK? In what way?" enquired Chingiz, caught off-guard.

"Just OK – the tea?"

"Oh, fine, it's wonderful tea. Thank you."

Looking slightly bemused, Chingiz tried to find the thread of his last sentence, and once again was raising a head of verbal steam when she came back. He caught her in his peripheral vision and did a double-take.

"Is everything still OK?" she asked, and Chingiz nodded vigorously, the smile more forced now. In fact, he had not yet touched the tea. But she didn't move.

"Where is that man from?" she then asked, looking at Chingiz, but moving her eyes back and forth in my direction. This was testing my friend's patience, I could tell, but I had understood the question, and so I responded, "America."

"Oh, that's amazing," she said, her eyes wide and the smile reaching even greater proportions. She then proceeded to grill Chingiz about what I did, why I was there, etc. He entered into the spirit of the thing, and once more, she retreated.

---

38 Tea is served in glass cups in Azerbaijan, and a pot is not a normal visitor to a restaurant table.

"I hope she is not annoying you?" he enquired.

"Not at all, She has the liveliest face and most open expression I have ever seen – how could she possibly annoy anyone? To tell you the truth, she has me under her spell!"

"I agree, and she is certainly very different from the normal waitress. But, by the way, I never asked you whether you wanted anything to eat."

By this time I was ready for a snack, but the anticipation of the long night, and even longer flight, did not push my hunger beyond snack level.

"What I would really like," I responded, "is a dessert, something sweet. I am in the mood for that right now."

He started to rise, and I informed him that there was no need to disturb himself because I was *quite certain* that the waitress would be back *tout de suite*. She was indeed there before the thought was out of my head. Chingiz by now had caught the humour in this situation, and was smiling – his eyes glinting – as he prepared to make his request for dessert.

"May I see his ring?" she asked, stopping Chingiz in midbreath before he could utter a word.

"Pardon?" he asked, confused.

"He has such a beautiful ring, I was wondering if I might see it."

I took off my ring, and with a smile that was a miserable substitute for hers, I handed it to her. She examined it, and then reached out and slowly slid it back on my finger – her eyes never leaving mine. By now, Chingiz was completely caught up in the singularity of this whole performance.

"Do you have any dessert?" he enquired, breaking the magic spell.

"No, but I can get some from the store if you want it," she offered animatedly, the eyes now wide and sparkling.

We informed her that if she would do that, we would be most grateful, and off she went.

It was quite some time before she reappeared, and Chingiz and I were back into earnest exchange when suddenly she ran into the room, face flushed and clearly out of breath. In a gesture of triumph, she banged a box onto the table between us, and Chingiz shot upright. She was doubled over like a hurdler after a race. Both of us leaned forward simultaneously to examine the box, to find that it contained an entire, very large Swiss roll. I happen to like Swiss roll, so I was a happy man.

"This is wonderful!" I exclaimed, and she straightened up as Chingiz told her of my delight. She clapped her hands together.

Chingiz then looked at the waitress, matching her smile for smile – for he is no weakling in the charm department himself – as he informed her that we couldn't eat it right out of the box. She switched from joy to deep concern, grabbed the box, and rushed out. I became nervous about the fate of my hastily removed Swiss roll, and was beginning to enter the anxiety-attack stage, when my good friend explained what he had asked her for.

The roll duly reappeared on a china plate, neatly sliced.

"It looks great," observed Chingiz, which earned us an even-more radiant beam. "But my friend needs a fork," and she was gone again.

When the fork and the spirit of the forest returned together, Chingiz turned, and, upping the ante, beamed his thanks at her. He turned back to me, recovered his train of thought and was just about to continue our fragmentary conversation when the waitress sat down next to me on my right hand side, her chin resting on one hand, her elbow on the table, and the other hand holding the fork. We were frozen in space, and were totally at a loss now, because it looked as though she was going to share our Swiss roll, which would certainly be a first for the Azerbaijan catering community. Chingiz, eyes wide, was facing me, locked in mid-word, looking from me to her, from her to me. It is very rare for anyone to upstage him, but he was totally out of his league here. She remained poised like a statue over the roll, and we realised that maybe she was waiting, out of politeness, for a signal, not wishing to plunge in before us. Neither of us, of course, possessed a fork, so she had a real advantage. Our conversation – whatever it was – was now ancient history.

"Oh, please start," Chingiz told her, polite as ever.

Neither of us, I will admit, was ready for what followed, for we had misjudged the situation and the forest elf completely. I was about to say something to Chingiz, while our new companion devoured her first slice. I opened my mouth, only to find a fork and a perfect circle of Swiss roll first in front of it and then firmly in it. Now, of course, I could say nothing until I swallowed. I turned, and there she was, elbow on the table, charging the fork for its next journey; eyes locked on mine.

Over the course of the next fifteen minutes, she fed me *every slice* of the Swiss roll, sometimes playing aeroplanes with the fork before popping the slice in my mouth, much as a mother would do with a baby that is noticing things for the first time. The situation was admirably reflected by the look on Chingiz' face – wonderment would describe it well. Periodically she asked him if I was enjoying it, and there was no denying my delight. His eyes followed every move of the fork. He was captivated.

Eventually, the roll all gone, she put down the fork and quietly took everything away. The time had come for us to leave, even though she had charmed the boots off both of us.

"Do you want another?" Chingiz enquired, laughing.

We explained sadly that we would have loved to stay, but I had a plane to catch. Chingiz explained what a wonderful and unexpected evening we had had, *all* due to our charming waitress. She blushed, and then, wound up like a spring, followed us out of the room, across the roof, to the top of the stairs that wound down three flights to the exit. We shook her hand, and thanked her warmly.

There she stood, at the top of the stairs, behind the short balustrade, watching us descend each step of the stairs to the first landing. At that place, we turned to wave at her, and she looked like she was thinking desperately, her eyebrows knotted, eyes closed, her hands over her cheeks. We waited, wondering if she was all right, but suddenly her face opened and lit up. She leaned over the balcony, and in beautiful English she said clearly and loudly, to me:

"I LOVE YOU."

Chingiz went into shock.

"And I love you too," I shouted back with a smile. She went beetroot red and waved, and watched us every step of the way.

"I have lived in Baku well over thirty years," said a beaming Chingiz as we strolled through the Old City. "That was a first."

"Believe me, it was a first for me too," I said, and we both laughed, disturbing 600 years of sleeping architecture.

17

Strange doings in Terre Haute

INDIANA, 2004

I HAD JUST succeeded in locking myself out of my 1977 Cadillac Biarritz in the historic downtown district of Terre Haute, Indiana. To remedy this situation, my son Eldar was doing amazing things with a yard of bent wire, while his wife Jami stood on the porch.

"I hope he is not going to be too long with that," she said, looking both concerned and at her watch.

"Oh, don't worry, I can always call the Triple A (the American Automobile Association). We have plenty of time and there is no rush."

"No, there is – because there is something we found that made us say 'Randall has to see this and tell us what he thinks happened'."

That piqued my interest, and I went over to the car, as though my presence would suddenly make the wire jiggling any more effective. Abruptly, there was a loud *clunk*, and we were inside the 2.5 ton monster.

"OK, let's go. We don't want to be there after dark," Jami said, heading off and setting a brisk pace around the corner.

Our short walk soon brought us to what appeared to be a large, well-preserved brick house that still looked very solid, but was noticeably in the first stages of decline. Many of the window panes were smashed, but otherwise, and very curiously, the entire rest of the exterior looked as though it had been recently renovated. The garden, though guarded behind a low cast-iron fence, had long since gone back to Nature.

Taking me round the back of the house, Jami and Eldar showed me another curious conjunction: the rear door was hanging crazily off, revealing a welter of rubbish in the small foyer beyond; and yet two black bags had been set out ready to go to the kerb for collection, but had never made it. Beyond the open doorway as we entered, we saw two staircases. The first, directly ahead of us, led down into a spacious basement, where building equipment and tools lay mouldering under a layer of dust. On the other short staircase, which led in a reverse 'L' shape up into the main part of the house, all sorts of litter was scattered: stamp albums, personal papers and the like.

Having ascended the two short flights of stairs to our right, we entered a fine Victorian room that had been carefully decorated with very expensive reproduction period wallpaper. From the ceiling in the centre of the room hung a chandelier, clearly new, and to the right was a well-appointed cast-iron refurbished Victorian fireplace. The floor was extremely fine narrow-blocked hardwood with a glorious patina of age, and as tight as a drum. So it was clear that, whenever the windows had been broken, it had not happened before last winter (this intrusion of ours being in June), as there was no sign of damp, mould, distortion or decay. But what did mar the effect of this partly renovated, though still empty, room were the obscenities that someone had spray-painted over the beautiful, and clearly new, wallpaper.

Moving through a fine arch, we entered what was clearly the main living and receiving room of the house, given its grand size, fine wainscoting, and large bay windows. Once again great effort and expenditure were evident in the painted woodwork and the expensive reproduction period wallpaper. The floor had a different, and very beautiful, configuration of hardwood, once again in splendid condition, and in one corner it supported an upright piano. This stood perpendicular to a fine porphyry Victorian fireplace of grand dimensions, and the whole room, though a little dark, benefited from wonderful wood panelling. Here and there were tools and human artefacts, and once more a brand new light fitting hung over the centre of the room.

Once more, delinquents with spray cans had trashed the painstaking restoration work.

The next room, which was considerably smaller, was strewn with a vast accumulation of personal papers, including bank statements and student-loan accounts, tax information and all those things that you would be foolish to let out of your sight. Indeed, all manner of personal things were here, including books on pregnancy, company documents relating to the work of a sales representative, travel planners, and more. The documentation clearly indicated a young married couple expecting, or in possession of, a child. Their name was on all the envelopes, though it will be left in anonymity here, along with the address of this residence. The correspondence, such as we were able to find, went up to somewhere around April 2003 – a little over one year earlier. There were also toys for an infant, and all manner of letters and cards. All this was dumped in a heap on the floor around the door, and there was no clear indication where it could have been before that. But all the correspondence was completely 'normal', without any signs of pressure, foreclosure, etc. It portrayed a well-ordered daily pattern of routine events in the lives of a young couple moving into a new, if somewhat vast, home. But where were they? It all stopped dead, at one point.

"It's like the *Mary Celeste*," I observed, though there were no unfinished meals.

On the next floor up, in another partly-finished room, we found a new restraining seat for a small infant to be secured into a car. It lay on its back on the floor – like everything else, abandoned. Again I puzzled why, since people had clearly been into the house, it had not been stripped. This curious fact was emphasised in every bathroom, for they had all been 'retro-modernised' with expensive reproduction Victorian fittings and brass taps. There was even soap in the soap dish. Some of these fittings were not yet plumbed in, so their removal was simply a matter of lift and leave. But the layer of dust indicated how long they had been standing there, waiting for something to happen.

It was all so intriguing because it had none of the impression of a job that had had to be stopped for lack of funds. Rather, it had the appearance of a job that had, perforce, stopped when the people concerned vanished from the face of the earth – and some time ago. Ivy was already growing in prodigiously through the broken window panes around the eaves, and one winter would see the end of this beautiful house, with its wonderful woodwork and all the effort that someone had put in to renovate it.

After viewing a new room that was in the process of being added, we stopped in confusion.

"So what do you think happened?" daughter-in-law Jami asked.

"We should think it out as the good Mr Holmes would have done," I suggested, because it did seem to have the making of a peculiarly good mystery. Putting together what we had seen,

I ventured: "First, we already agree that the owners did not decide that the costs of the renovation were excessive because it would make absolutely no sense, even if that were the case, to totally *abandon* the house.[39] That would be absurd as they would then be in possession of a wasting and deteriorating asset."

"So you don't think they just went broke?" enquired son Eldar.

"No, the situation we see here – to me at least – would seem to be totally illogical, even if they did," I countered.

"But don't you think the bank foreclosed on him?" Eldar asked.

"No, because he seems to be in good standing on his payments, according to that paperwork back there, and there was also material from his job as a company representative, plus he had a student loan so I don't think he was in financial difficulty, or was a financial problem for anyone else. Plus, if the bank had foreclosed on him, there would be a For Sale sign in the yard, and there isn't one."

"No, I pass here often," said Jami. "There has never been a sign."

"And," I added, "if the bank had foreclosed, they would have to be idiots to let this happen to the only asset to come out of the bad loan. As Spock would say, 'It doesn't compute'."

"So that rules out the bank." Jami commented.

"Well then, maybe they got transferred?" Eldar enquired.

"Even if they did, they would try to sell the property because it is theirs to sell, and there has never been a 'For Sale' sign, as Jami said. Otherwise, they would still be paying the mortgage on this house from their new location; and meanwhile it is falling to bits. Plus, why would you leave all your personal papers, the child's toys, and the car seat? Those are not things you would leave behind if you were resettled, except possibly

---

39 It should be remembered that this was before the recession, and houses were accumulating value rapidly and selling well.

in the Witness-Protection Programme. You do not walk out of the door and leave all your personal things behind."

"Also," I went on, "it seems clear that there was a child in this family: a new child. Of course, we have all the books on pregnancy, etc., but the car seat sort of suggests to me that the baby had arrived – but also the seat has been lying there abandoned for some time, as you can see from the dust."

Still perplexed, we walked round the remainder of the rooms, and it was the same story of renovation of a very solid house yielding to total abandonment and decay.

"The real central point of this mystery here, it seems to me," I suggested, "is the fact that the house is not for sale. Nobody in their right mind would, or could afford to, let this happen. In a couple of years it will be ruined. We know the owners had bought it, and they could not afford to walk away from it. We know it is not for sale. Is there any situation that would fit these facts?"

We all pondered for a while, and concluded that none of it made sense. Then Jami chimed in with the remark, "Did you see the concrete plaque on the wall above the side door?"

"No," we chimed. "What does it say?"

"Well," she responded, "it looks like the name of a restaurant. The plaque, even though it is overgrown now by ivy, looks new."

She was absolutely right, and so this was to have been a period tearoom, hence the efforts at recreating a true Victorian feel. I could not see any way, though, that this would change the basic argument.

"What do you think?" they asked.

"What do I think? Sadly, I have to say that my instinct is that the former young inhabitants of this house are dead. To my way of thinking, it's the only explanation that fits. Why does everything stop all of a sudden – the *Mary Celeste* thing? Why are personal effects left lying around – even *very* personal ones? Because, I suppose, nobody needs them any more."

Jami looked around at the house, with its splendid proportions, solid construction, excellent woodwork, and an air of graciousness, which we had all decided we would love to inhabit. I would have moved in there on the spot.

"Yes, but why doesn't *someone* sell it? Even if the original owners are dead, you know, someone, somewhere *must* own it?" Jami asked.

I thought about it and said, "You know, that is the one thing, above all, that convinces me that they are dead. I also think they died without leaving a will, which is not that uncommon with young people. No will meant that, when they *did* die, it was not clear *who* owned the property through inheritance. It has, even now, a very substantial value, and has had a *lot* of money spent on it. In those circumstances, unless the legal situation is resolved right away, *nobody* owns it formally, and for that reason, *nobody* is going to spend any money looking after it – not the lawyers, not the relatives, not even the potential beneficiaries. Why? Because they would have no guarantee of ever seeing a return on the investment. Only that, to my mind, would explain why a perfectly good and very desirable house like this would be allowed to go to Hell."

"You think they are all dead? How do you think they died?" Jami asked.

"Who knows?" I responded, "My guess would be something like a car crash, and they all died together."

"No, not *all*," said Jami, grabbing our attention.

"How can you possibly know that?" I asked.

"Because the baby's car seat is upstairs on the floor," she responded. "If the baby had been in the car, Indiana law requires him or her to be strapped into that."

"You are better at the Holmes stuff that I am," I admitted freely. "I had totally forgotten that. Well, then if that is the case, I guess the baby owns it – but I am no lawyer."

"But you know what?" Jami asked with concern.

"No, what?" I enquired, wondering what new insight was about to break forth.

"If you think I am staying in this house once it gets dark, you have another think coming. Especially after what we have just decided. I think it's time for some Italian food," she said, to a solidly appreciative husband and a similarly inclined father-in-law.

"I'll tell you one thing for sure," Eldar observed. "This place is creepy, and that's why we thought you would like it. I guess we could find out, now we know their names, the date the last letter was delivered, you know?"

"Yes, probably from the local newspaper, their insurance company, the title office – there are many possibilities. But you know what? Sometimes it is good to have a little mystery in our lives. After all, we never did find out how the entire crew and the captain's family vanished from the *Mary Celeste*. And, if we did, who would ever care to hear of it again?"[40]

---

40 One more mystery, The ship was called the *Mary Celeste*, but Conan Doyle got it wrong when he wrote the story: assuming that if the second name was French, the first name must be French too, he referred to it as the *Marie Celeste*.

Also from Y Lolfa:

£9.99